THIS BOOK BELONGS TO

The Library of

....

....

I can't tell you how grateful I am that you decided to read my book. My most heartfelt thanks that you took time out of your life to choose my work and I hope you find benefit within these pages.

There are so many books available today that offer similar content so that makes it even more humbling that you decided to buying mine.

Tell me what you thought! I am eager to hear your opinion and ideas on what you read as are others who are looking for a good book to buy. Leave a review on Amazon.com so others can benefit from your wisdom!

With much thanks.

Table of Contents

SUMMARY

Portrait drawing is an art form that has captivated artists and art enthusiasts for centuries. The allure of portrait drawing lies in its ability to capture the essence and personality of a subject, creating a visual representation that goes beyond mere physical likeness. It allows the artist to delve into the depths of human emotions, expressions, and experiences, and convey them through the strokes of a pencil or brush.

One of the main reasons why portrait drawing is so appealing is its intimate nature. Unlike other forms of art, such as landscape or still life, portrait drawing involves a direct interaction between the artist and the subject. This interaction allows the artist to observe and study the subject's features, expressions, and body language, enabling them to create a more accurate and lifelike representation. The process of capturing the unique characteristics of an individual's face can be both challenging and rewarding, as it requires a keen eye for detail and a deep understanding of human anatomy.

Furthermore, portrait drawing offers a platform for self-expression and storytelling. Through the careful selection of composition, lighting, and pose, an artist can convey a narrative or evoke a specific mood in their portrait. Whether it's a somber expression that reflects the subject's inner turmoil or a joyful smile that radiates happiness, portrait drawing allows the artist to communicate emotions and stories that words alone cannot capture. This ability to communicate on a deeper level is what makes portrait drawing such a powerful and compelling art form.

In addition to its expressive qualities, portrait drawing also serves as a means of preserving memories and capturing a moment in time. Portraits have been used throughout history to immortalize individuals, whether they are famous figures or loved ones. They serve as a visual record of a person's existence, allowing future generations to connect with their ancestors and gain insight into their lives. The ability to create a lasting legacy through portrait drawing is a significant aspect of its allure.

Moreover, portrait drawing offers a unique challenge for artists, as it requires a combination of technical skill and artistic interpretation. Achieving a likeness in a portrait involves mastering the intricacies of proportion, shading, and perspective, while also infusing the artwork with the artist's personal style and vision. This balance between technical accuracy and creative expression is what sets portrait drawing apart from other art forms and makes it a rewarding pursuit for artists of all levels.

Understanding the human face is a complex and fascinating topic that has intrigued scientists, psychologists, and artists for centuries. The face is not only a means of communication and expression, but it also plays a crucial role in our social interactions and relationships. From a scientific perspective, studying the human face involves delving into various disciplines such as anatomy, physiology, psychology, and even computer science.

Anatomy is a fundamental aspect of understanding the human face. It involves examining the structure and composition of the face, including the bones, muscles, and skin. The face is composed of numerous bones, such as the skull, mandible, and maxilla, which provide the framework for the facial features. The muscles of the face are responsible for the wide range of expressions we can make, from smiling to frowning, and they work in harmony to convey our emotions and intentions. Additionally, the skin of the face is unique in its sensitivity and ability to stretch and contract, allowing for facial movements and expressions.

Physiology also plays a significant role in understanding the human face. It involves studying the functions and processes that occur within the face, such as blood circulation, nerve signaling, and sensory perception. For example, the blood vessels in the face supply oxygen and nutrients to the skin and muscles, giving the face its healthy and vibrant appearance. Nerve signaling allows us to feel sensations on our face, such as touch, temperature, and pain, and it also enables us to control our facial muscles for expression and communication.

Psychology is another crucial aspect of understanding the human face. It involves exploring the cognitive and emotional processes that occur when we perceive and interpret facial expressions. The face is a powerful tool for communication, as it can convey a wide range of emotions, intentions, and social cues. Through facial expressions, we can express happiness, sadness, anger, fear, and many other emotions, allowing others to understand our internal states. Additionally, our ability to recognize and interpret facial expressions in others is essential for empathy, social bonding, and understanding the emotions of those around us.

Advancements in technology, particularly in the field of computer science, have also contributed to our understanding of the human face. Computer vision and facial recognition algorithms have been developed to analyze and interpret facial features, expressions, and identities. These technologies have applications in various fields, such as security, entertainment, and healthcare. They allow for the detection of emotions, identification of individuals, and even the creation of realistic virtual avatars.

The preliminary sketch is the initial representation or draft of a design or artwork. It serves as a starting point for the artist or designer to visualize their ideas and concepts before proceeding with the final version. This stage is crucial as it allows for experimentation, exploration, and refinement of the overall composition, proportions, and elements of the artwork.

In terms of visual art, a preliminary sketch can be a rough drawing or a series of quick sketches that capture the basic shapes, lines, and forms of the subject matter. It helps the artist establish the overall composition, determine the placement of objects or figures, and test different perspectives or viewpoints. This initial sketch acts as a guide for the artist to develop and refine their ideas further.

For design projects, such as architecture or product design, a preliminary sketch is often a more detailed representation of the proposed concept. It may include annotations, measurements, and notes to communicate specific design elements or functionalities. This sketch serves as a visual communication tool between the designer and the client or team members, allowing for feedback and adjustments before moving forward with the final design.

The preliminary sketch is not meant to be a finished or polished artwork. It is a rough representation that captures the essence of the artist's or designer's vision. It provides a starting point for further development and refinement, allowing for adjustments and modifications to be made based on feedback and creative decisions.

Overall, the preliminary sketch is a crucial step in the creative process. It allows artists and designers to explore their ideas, experiment with different compositions or concepts, and communicate their vision to others. It serves as a foundation for the final artwork or design, guiding the artist or designer towards achieving their desired outcome.

Understanding light and shadow is a fundamental concept in the field of physics and plays a crucial role in various aspects of our daily lives. Light is a form of electromagnetic radiation that enables us to see the world around us, while shadow is the absence of light caused by an object blocking the path of light rays.

To comprehend light and shadow, it is essential to understand the nature of light itself. Light is composed of tiny particles called photons, which travel in waves. These waves have different properties, such as wavelength and frequency, which determine the characteristics of light. The wavelength of light determines its color, with shorter wavelengths corresponding to colors like blue and violet, and longer wavelengths corresponding to colors like red and orange.

When light encounters an object, it can interact with it in several ways. One possibility is reflection, where light bounces off the surface of the object and changes direction. This is why we can see objects that are not directly in the path of light, as the reflected light reaches our eyes. Another possibility is absorption, where the object absorbs some or all of the light energy, converting it into other forms of energy, such as heat. The third possibility is transmission, where light passes through the object, allowing us to see objects on the other side.

Shadows are formed when an object blocks the path of light. When light rays hit an opaque object, they cannot pass through it, resulting in the formation of a shadow on the opposite side of the object. The size and shape of the shadow depend on the position and size of the light source, as well as the distance between the object and the surface on which the shadow is cast. Shadows can also be influenced by the shape and texture of the object casting the shadow, as well as the angle at which the light rays hit the object.

Understanding light and shadow has numerous practical applications. In art and photography, knowledge of light and shadow is crucial for creating realistic and visually appealing images. By understanding how light interacts with different surfaces and objects, artists and photographers can manipulate lighting conditions to achieve desired effects and convey specific moods or emotions.

In architecture and interior design, understanding light and shadow is essential for creating well-lit and visually pleasing spaces. By strategically placing windows, skylights, and artificial lighting sources, architects and designers can control the amount and quality of light in a room, enhancing its functionality and aesthetics.

When it comes to drawing eyes, lips, and brows, there are various techniques that can be employed to achieve realistic and captivating results. These facial features play a crucial role in conveying emotions and expressions in any artwork, so it is essential to pay attention to the details and master the techniques involved.

Starting with the eyes, they are often considered the windows to the soul and can greatly enhance the overall appearance of a drawing. To begin, it is important to understand the basic structure of the eye. The eye consists of the iris, pupil, eyelids, eyelashes, and the surrounding area known as the eye socket. By studying the anatomy of the eye, artists can accurately depict its shape and proportions.

One technique for drawing eyes is to start with a basic oval shape to outline the eye socket. From there, the iris and pupil can be added, taking into consideration the direction and intensity of the light source to create realistic shading and highlights. Paying attention to the details such as the reflection in the eye and the texture of the iris can further enhance the realism of the drawing.

Moving on to the lips, they are another important feature that can greatly impact the overall expression of a drawing. To begin, it is helpful to outline the basic shape of the lips, taking into consideration factors such as the width, height, and curvature. Lips can vary greatly in shape and size, so it is important to observe and study different references to accurately depict them.

When shading the lips, it is important to consider the light source and the natural highlights and shadows that occur. Adding subtle details such as the cupid's bow, the texture of the lips, and the presence of wrinkles or creases can further enhance the realism of the drawing. Additionally, paying attention to the color and texture of the lips, such as whether they are glossy or matte, can add depth and dimension to the artwork.

Lastly, the brows are often referred to as the frame of the face and can greatly impact the overall expression and appearance of a drawing. To begin, it is important to observe and study different brow shapes and sizes to accurately depict them. Brows can vary greatly in thickness, arch, and length, so it is important to pay attention to these details.

When shading the brows, it is important to consider the direction and intensity of the light source to create realistic shadows and highlights. Adding subtle details such as individual brow hairs and the presence of gaps or sparse areas can further enhance the realism of the drawing.

The input working on fine details refers to the act of focusing on and paying close attention to the small and intricate aspects of a task or project. This could apply to various fields and activities, such as art, design, writing, engineering, or any other endeavor that requires precision and meticulousness.

When someone is working on fine details, they are typically engaged in a process that involves scrutinizing every element and aspect of their work. This could involve examining minute details, making subtle adjustments, or refining specific features to achieve a desired outcome. It often requires a high level of concentration, patience, and a keen eye for detail.

In the context of art or design, working on fine details could involve adding intricate patterns, textures, or shading to enhance the overall visual appeal of a piece. Artists may spend hours meticulously applying brushstrokes or using fine tools to create intricate designs or textures. Similarly, designers may focus on perfecting the alignment, spacing, and typography of elements in a layout to ensure a visually pleasing and cohesive design.

In the realm of writing, working on fine details could involve carefully editing and proofreading a piece of writing to ensure grammatical accuracy, clarity, and coherence. Writers may scrutinize each sentence, word choice, and punctuation mark to refine their work and convey their intended message effectively. They may also pay attention to the flow and structure of their writing, ensuring that each paragraph and section seamlessly transitions and contributes to the overall narrative or argument.

In engineering or technical fields, working on fine details could involve meticulously analyzing and refining complex systems or designs. Engineers may spend significant time examining intricate components, conducting precise calculations, or conducting thorough testing to ensure the functionality, safety, and efficiency of their creations. They may also focus on optimizing performance, reducing errors, or improving the overall user experience through careful attention to detail.

Overall, working on fine details is a crucial aspect of many disciplines and activities. It is a process that requires patience, precision, and a commitment to excellence. By dedicating time and effort to refining the small and intricate aspects of their work, individuals can achieve a higher level of quality, professionalism, and satisfaction in their final outcomes.

A comprehensive analysis of case studies featuring renowned portrait artists, highlighting their unique styles, techniques, and contributions to the art world.

Introduction:

Portrait art has been a significant genre throughout the history of art, capturing the essence and personality of individuals through various mediums and styles. This analysis aims to delve into the case studies of renowned portrait artists, shedding light on their artistic journeys, techniques, and the impact they have made on the art world.

Case Study 1: Leonardo da Vinci

Leonardo da Vinci, a true Renaissance polymath, is widely regarded as one of the greatest portrait artists in history. His iconic portrait, the Mona Lisa, is a testament to his mastery of capturing the enigmatic expressions and emotions of his subjects. Da Vinci's meticulous attention to detail, his use of sfumato (a technique that creates a smoky, hazy effect), and his ability to infuse a sense of depth and realism into his portraits set him apart from his contemporaries. His innovative approach to portraiture revolutionized the genre and continues to inspire artists to this day.

Case Study 2: Frida Kahlo

Frida Kahlo, a Mexican artist known for her self-portraits, used her art as a medium to express her innermost emotions and struggles. Her unique style, characterized by vibrant colors, surreal elements, and symbolic imagery, allowed her to convey her physical and emotional pain resulting from a tragic accident and a tumultuous personal life. Kahlo's self-portraits are not merely representations of her physical appearance but serve as a window into her psyche, making her one of the most influential portrait artists of the 20th century.

Case Study 3: Rembrandt van Rijn

Rembrandt van Rijn, a Dutch master of the 17th century, is renowned for his ability to capture the human soul in his portraits. His use of chiaroscuro, a technique that emphasizes the contrast between light and dark, adds a sense of drama and depth to his works. Rembrandt's portraits often depict his subjects in a contemplative state, revealing their inner thoughts and emotions. His ability to convey the complexities of human nature through his brushstrokes and his mastery of capturing the play of light and shadow make him a true pioneer in the field of portrait art.

Case Study 4: Pablo Picasso

Pablo Picasso, a Spanish artist who co-founded the Cubist movement, revolutionized the concept of portraiture by deconstructing and

A digital portrait drawing is a form of art that involves creating a realistic or stylized representation of a person's face using digital tools and software. It is a popular medium among artists, as it allows for greater flexibility and experimentation compared to traditional methods like pencil or paint.

To create a digital portrait drawing, an artist typically starts by sketching the basic outline of the face using a digital pen or stylus on a graphics tablet. They then proceed to add more details, such as facial features, hair, and clothing, using various digital brushes and tools available in the software.

One of the advantages of digital portrait drawing is the ability to easily correct mistakes or make changes without damaging the original artwork. Artists can simply undo or erase any unwanted elements and try different techniques until they achieve the desired result. This flexibility allows for greater experimentation and exploration of different styles and approaches.

Another advantage of digital portrait drawing is the ability to work with layers. Layers are like transparent sheets that can be stacked on top of each other, allowing artists to separate different elements of the drawing and make adjustments independently. For example, an artist can create a separate layer for the background, the face, and the hair, making it easier to modify each element without affecting the rest of the drawing.

Digital portrait drawing also offers a wide range of tools and effects that can enhance the overall appearance of the artwork. Artists can use various brushes to create different textures and shading techniques, giving the drawing a more realistic or stylized look. They can also experiment with different color palettes and lighting effects to create a specific mood or atmosphere.

In addition to its artistic benefits, digital portrait drawing also offers practical advantages. The digital format allows for easy sharing and reproduction of the artwork, making it accessible to a wider audience. Artists can easily print their digital drawings or share them online through social media platforms or websites.

Overall, digital portrait drawing is a versatile and exciting medium that combines traditional art techniques with the advantages of digital technology. It offers artists greater flexibility, experimentation, and the ability to create stunning and realistic or stylized representations of people's faces. Whether it's for personal enjoyment, professional commissions, or commercial purposes, digital portrait drawing is a popular choice among artists and art enthusiasts alike.

Telling a story through portraits is a captivating and powerful way to convey a narrative. Portraits have long been used as a means of capturing the essence of a person, their emotions, and their experiences. By carefully selecting subjects, settings, and compositions, a photographer or artist can create a series of portraits that collectively tell a story.

Each portrait within the series can represent a different chapter or moment in the narrative. The subjects themselves can be individuals or groups, each with their own unique story to tell. Through their facial expressions, body language, and the way they interact with their surroundings, the viewer can gain insight into their lives and experiences.

The setting and composition of each portrait also play a crucial role in storytelling. The background, props, and lighting can all contribute to the overall mood and atmosphere of the image, helping to convey the emotions and themes of the narrative. For example, a portrait taken in a dimly lit room with a somber expression on the subject's face may suggest a story of sadness or introspection, while a portrait taken in a vibrant outdoor setting with a joyful expression may suggest a story of happiness or celebration.

Furthermore, the sequencing and arrangement of the portraits within the series can further enhance the storytelling aspect. By carefully considering the order in which the portraits are presented, the artist can create a sense of progression and development in the narrative. This can be achieved through the use of visual cues, such as changes in lighting, composition, or the expressions of the subjects. By strategically placing certain portraits next to each other, the artist can create connections and contrasts between the different stories being told.

Telling a story through portraits allows for a deep exploration of the human experience. It allows the viewer to connect with the subjects on a personal level, to empathize with their joys and sorrows, and to gain a deeper understanding of the universal themes that bind us all together. Whether it is a series of portraits documenting a community, a family, or an individual's journey, the power of storytelling through portraits lies in its ability to evoke emotions, provoke thought, and inspire empathy.

Selling portrait art can be a challenging task, but with the right tips and strategies, you can increase your chances of success. Here are some detailed tips to help you sell your portrait art effectively:

1. Define your target audience: Before you start selling your portrait art, it's important to identify your target audience. Determine who would be interested in purchasing your artwork, whether it's individuals, families, pet owners, or businesses. Understanding your target audience will help you tailor your marketing efforts and create artwork that appeals to their preferences.

2. Showcase your portfolio: Building a strong portfolio is crucial for selling portrait art. Include a variety of your best work, showcasing different styles, subjects, and mediums. Make sure your portfolio is well-organized and visually appealing, as it will be the first impression potential buyers have of your art.

3. Utilize online platforms: In today's digital age, online platforms provide a great opportunity to reach a wider audience. Create a website or an online store to showcase and sell your portrait art. Additionally, consider utilizing social media platforms like Instagram, Facebook, or Pinterest to share your artwork and engage with potential buyers.

4. Attend art exhibitions and fairs: Participating in art exhibitions and fairs can help you gain exposure and connect with art enthusiasts and potential buyers. Research local art events and apply to showcase your artwork. Make sure to have business cards or brochures available to provide interested buyers with more information about your art.

5. Collaborate with local businesses: Partnering with local businesses can be mutually beneficial. Approach cafes, restaurants, or galleries to display your artwork on their walls. This not only provides exposure for your art but also gives potential buyers a chance to see your work in person. Offer a commission to the business for any sales made through their establishment.

6. Offer customization options: Providing customization options can attract more buyers. Offer to create personalized portraits based on specific requests or preferences. This could include incorporating specific colors, backgrounds, or even adding additional elements to the portrait. Customization adds value to your artwork and makes it more appealing to potential buyers.

7. Provide excellent customer service: Building a positive reputation is crucial for selling portrait art. Ensure you provide excellent customer service throughout the entire sales process. Respond promptly to inquiries, be professional and friendly, and go the extra mile to meet your customers'

expectations. Satisfied customers are more likely to recommend your art to others and become repeat buyers.

I hope this message finds you well. I wanted to take a moment to reach out and offer you some words of encouragement as you continue on your journey of self-improvement.

Firstly, I want to commend you for your dedication and commitment to bettering yourself. It takes a great deal of courage and determination to recognize areas in our lives that need improvement and actively work towards making positive changes. Your willingness to embark on this journey is truly inspiring.

I want you to know that progress is not always linear. There may be times when you feel like you're taking two steps forward and one step back, and that's completely normal. Remember that setbacks and obstacles are a natural part of the growth process. It's important to be patient with yourself and not get discouraged when things don't go as planned. Instead, view these challenges as opportunities for learning and growth.

It's also crucial to celebrate your achievements, no matter how small they may seem. Each step forward, no matter how tiny, is a step in the right direction. Take the time to acknowledge and appreciate the progress you've made so far. Recognize the effort and hard work you've put in, and let it fuel your motivation to keep going.

Surrounding yourself with a supportive network of friends, family, or mentors can also be incredibly beneficial. Having people who believe in you and your potential can provide the encouragement and motivation you need during moments of doubt. Lean on them for support, seek their guidance, and share your successes and challenges with them. Remember, you don't have to go through this journey alone.

Lastly, I want to remind you to be kind to yourself. Self-improvement is a lifelong process, and it's important to practice self-compassion along the way. Treat yourself with the same kindness and understanding you would offer to a dear friend. Embrace your imperfections and mistakes as opportunities for growth, rather than reasons to be hard on yourself.

I have no doubt that you have the strength and determination to continue improving and reaching your goals. Believe in yourself and your abilities, and never lose sight of the progress you've already made. Keep pushing forward, and remember that each day is a new opportunity to become the best version of yourself.

Disclaimer

While all attempts have been made to verify the information provided in this book, the author does assume any responsibility for errors, omissions, or contrary interpretations of the subject matter contained within. The information provided in this book is for educational and entertainment purposes only. The reader is responsible for his or her own actions and the author does not accept any responsibilities for any liabilities or damages, real or perceived, resulting from the use of this information.

The trademarks that are used are without any consent, and the publication of the trademark is without permission or backing by the trademark owner. All trademarks and brands within this book are for clarifying purposes only and are the owned by the owners themselves, not affiliated with this document.

Introduction

Drawing human faces is considered as the most complicated part of sketching. However, no feat is difficult to achieve if you practice deliberately. Becoming an expert is drawing is just like becoming the master of any other sport. Every sportsperson starts the journey of learning one day and gradually learns the tricks and tips of the game. Similarly, if you give appropriate time and dedication to drawing portraits, nothing can stop you. Practically, learning portrait sketching does not take more than a month.

The first few days can be dedicated to learning basic outline drawing of the face and its features. Then, you can proceed to refining these features. In the first few chapters of this book, you will find guidance to draw the facial features, particularly eyes and hairs, in detail. In the forthcoming chapters, you will find different portraits of females and males. One chapter is particularly bestowed to the drawing of facial features in complete details. It will give you a closer look to the depth of eyes, lips, and nose.

Even though the portraits given in this book are made using computer software, you can draw them using your own regular equipment for drawing. Normally, the following things are needed to start pencil drawing or charcoal drawing: pencils (2H to 8B), rubber eraser, cutter blade, charcoal stick, and a rag.

These basic things are needed to start your amazing journey to portrait drawing. Regarding the choice of drawing sheets, you do not have to go for fancy sheets. Just a bunch of A3 cartridge sheets is enough. These sheets are very good at depicting the gradations of charcoal.

At last, you just need to dedicate your time to portrait drawing. When you start drawing, a full- fledged portrait may take up to a week to complete, if you give an hour daily. However, when you become an expert at portrait drawing, you may complete a detailed sketch in just 4-5 hours at a stretch.

Do not wait for the right time to come when you would start drawing. This is the right time; just grab your stuff and sit down to draw.

Chapter 1
Basics of Portrait Drawing

Drawing portraits seems difficult no doubt, but it can be made easy provided you know the right tricks. You do not have to be a decade old artist to learn drawing portraits; only a few weeks of experience is enough. First, choose a photograph that is rich in content, implying that there are variations in contrast, tonal value and the photo must be shot or printed in high resolution. You might find it difficult to find such photograph on Internet. If that is the case, you may have to get a photograph click of yourself or of someone else. Do not start your beautiful journey with a photograph with low resolution.

If you have a digital photograph, make it black and white, or convert it into grayscale. Now, crop the picture to get the size of face you want and print it. You will be able to view the tonal values clearly. Look at the picture carefully and determine the source of light, facial feature including eyes, nose, teeth, lips, ears, hairs, etc. When the hairs are light in color, you have to draw shadows among them, which is known as negative space drawing.

Notice if there are any wrinkles. If they are there, it is good news as well as bad news for you. The good news is that wrinkles bring life to a portrait, but they are hard to draw. They are like deep valleys with irregular shading on each side. Eyes and ears have wide range of tonal value. You can either draw each shade separately, or give darker shades first and then erase the graphite to give highlights. In any case, you have to be very patient and have a vision.

Notice the clothing of your subject. If there are many variations in design and tonal value, you will have to invest even more time. Therefore, try to crop your portrait to a proportion that face covers most of the area and only a small amount of clothing is visible; though you cannot eliminate clothing.

How to draw eyes

Eyes in a portrait are the most expressive and most difficult thing to draw. But do not get disheartened, they can be easily learned. It is important to observe the eyes closely before you start drawing. There are significant differences in the lines of lower and upper eyelids. The closer you observe, the more likeliness will be achieved.

The upper eyelid always covers some portion of the iris. A common mistake beginners make is to draw the iris small and then fit in within sclera. The lower portion of the iris is very slightly covered by the lower eyelid. You need to consider these two elements when you draw the glassy shell of the eyes:

- The bright spark of the reflected light must be left blank/ un-shaded sheet of paper when you begin tonal drawing. It will be the brightest part of the eyes. When the pupil is drawn in contrast, this bright portion is further augmented.

- The iris consists of a variation of flecks and tones, which radiate in the middle of pupil. The iris is darker on its exterior edge and lightens on the interior creating a lucid effect.

The last step is to execute solidification in the socket of the eye and the surrounding region using gradations.

The upper eyelid throws a shadow that creates a dark curve on top of eyeball, which slowly softens into shaded area in the eye's corner. Graduated shading can be done to give details to the outline and give tonal variations to the eyelids along with the surrounding regions. Eyelashes and eyebrows are made of delicate, soft hairs. Therefore, draw them with precision and pay attention to their direction of growth.

How to draw hairs

After eyes, hairs are the trickiest portion of a portrait to draw. However, once you achieve the required skills, you will fall in love with drawing hairs. Begin drawing the hair with a base layer- start drawing the black region with charcoal, and then smooth it using the flat surface of an eraser. You can also use a cloth or tissue to smudge charcoal. Create the strands of the hairs by using an eraser cut from its corner. You can keep cutting a thin edge of the eraser until you are done with drawing strands of hairs.

The erased white lines appear as if light reflects on the hairs. Draw darker lines using charcoal and ensure that your lines should be as thin and narrow as possible. Even in the darkest portion you see in your reference photograph, there are some fine lines that depict strands of hair. If you leave a patch of charcoal in a particular area of the head, it will look really odd. You can make minor changes in the direction of strands since hairs give you slight scope of flexibility.

Chapter 2
Elements of a Face

Before you sit down to draw a portrait, you need to understand the basic anatomy of a face. We cannot state a fixed rule for drawing a portrait since every face is different and there are no fixed sizes for the eyes, nose, lips, or ears. However, you can have an approximate judgment where these facial features should be placed in the frame of a face.

Steps to draw a face

Draw the outline of the face you want to draw. Sketch a vertical line in the center of the face. Now, draw a halfway horizontal line between the lower base of the jaw and the apex of the head (where the hair ends on top of the head). This line will be used to place the eyes. Then, halfway between the chin and eyes, draw a line to place the nose. Halfway between the chin and the nose, draw a line to place the center of mouth. It is important to note that there is a distance of one eye between both eyes. The ears are usually as long as the distance between eyes and base of nose. The length of lips is equal to the distance between two irises of the eyes if they focus straight.

A few examples of face outlines

Face 1

This is the face of a woman and it is drawn as told in the instructions given above. The ears are not shown in this face.

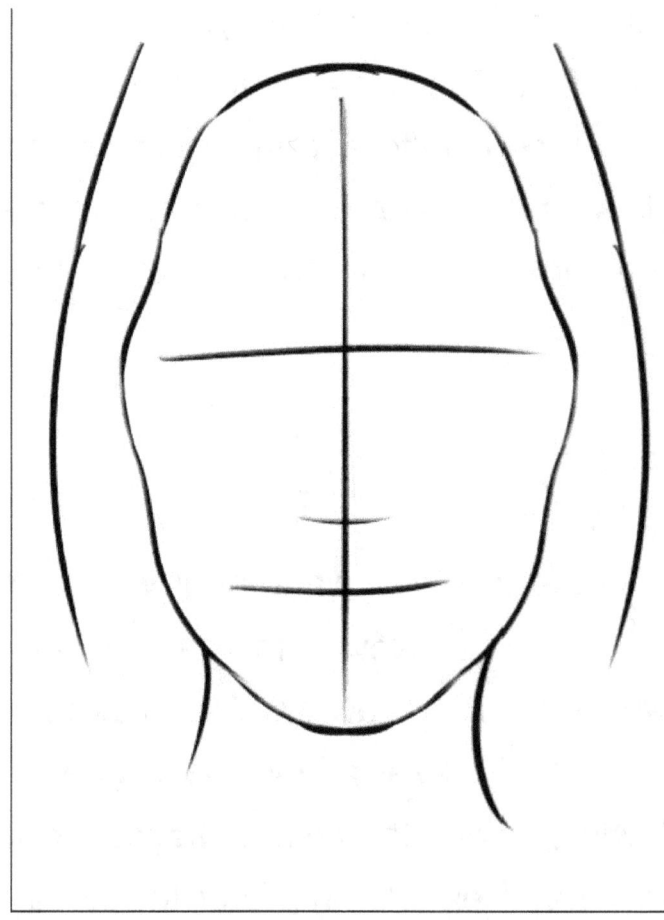

Face 2

This is the face of a young man. Here you can clearly see that the lower line for the placement of eyes is drawn exactly between the apex of the head and the lower base of chin. The other lines for the placement of facial features are also drawn as told above.

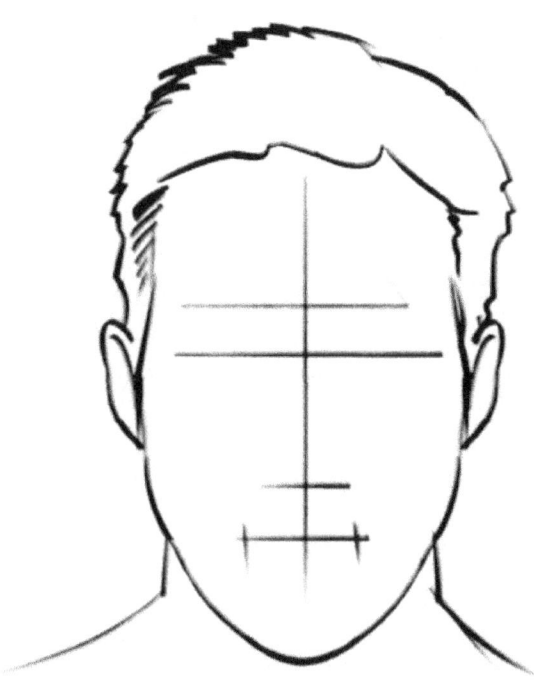

Face 3

This is the face of a teenager. Sometimes, you do not need many things to judge a face. The hairstyle of this boy is enough to say that this is going to be the portrait of a teenager or a man in his 20s.

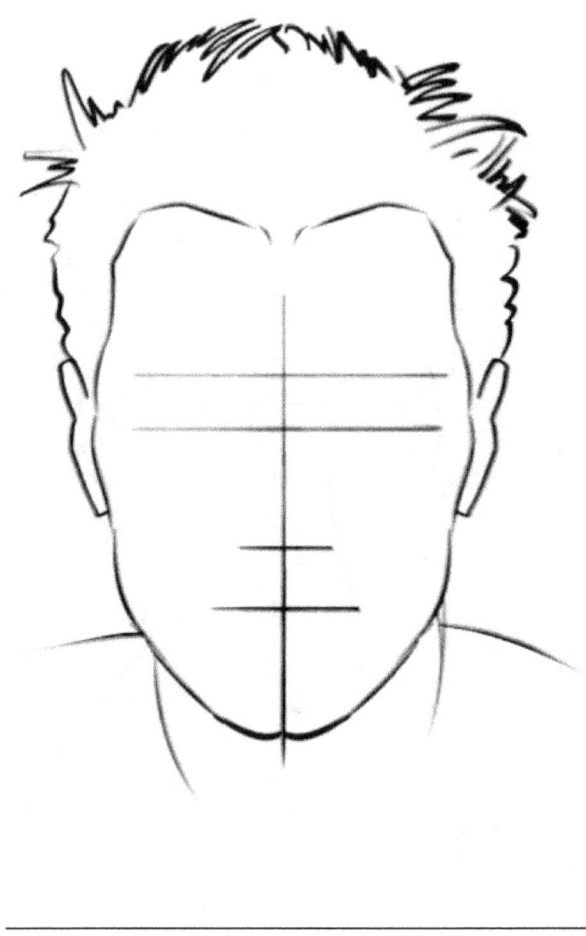

Eyes

Eyes are the most expressive feature of the face. They are capable of expressing hundreds of emotions just by little modifications. Let us go through a few expressions of eyes of males and females.

Eyes 1- hopeful eyes (female)

With a side-glance, this female is depicting hope in her eyes. Notice that the strands of eyebrows are drawn in different directions the eyelashes are also drawn in different lengths. If you observe closely, you will see fine white lines on the inner edge of the eyes, the sclera is not blank white, sclera consists of shadow cast by the upper eyelid, the reflection of light near the iris is blank white, there are different gradations within the eyeballs, and many more things.

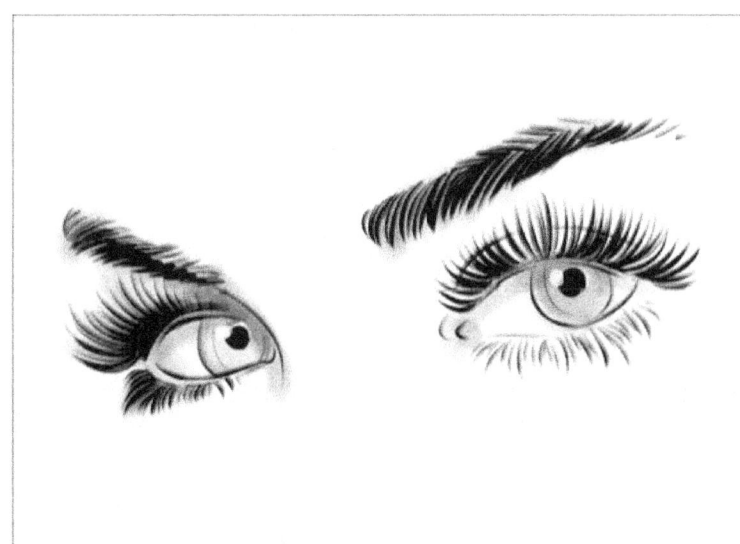

Eyes 2- sharp eyes (female)

This set of eyes also belongs to a female who is sharply looking at you. Just like the previous set of eyes, there are differences in different elements. No two set of eyes are same, therefore, you must carefully observe all the elements of an eye.

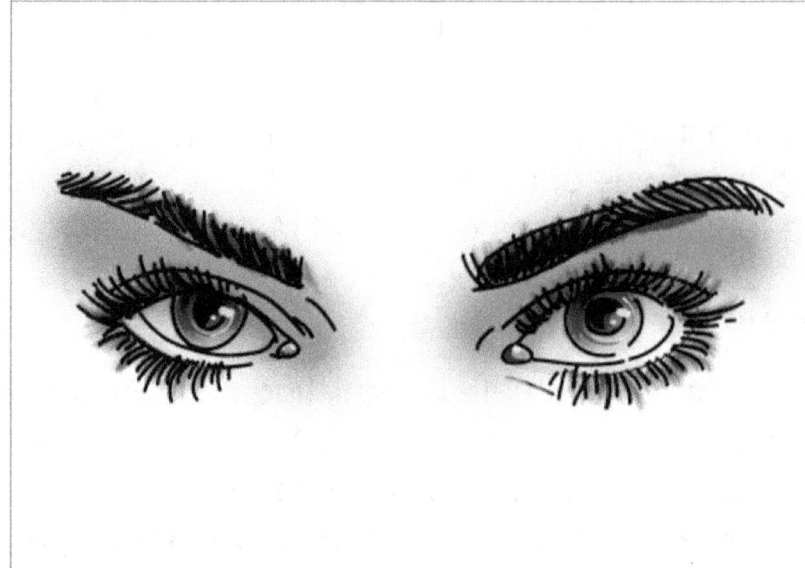

Eyes 3- irritated eyes (male)

The eyebrows of males are generally thicker than that of females. This man's eyes depict that he is irritated at something just by squinting his eyes a little. There is an arc under his right eye. You can use wrinkles around the eyes to depict age and expressions of a person.

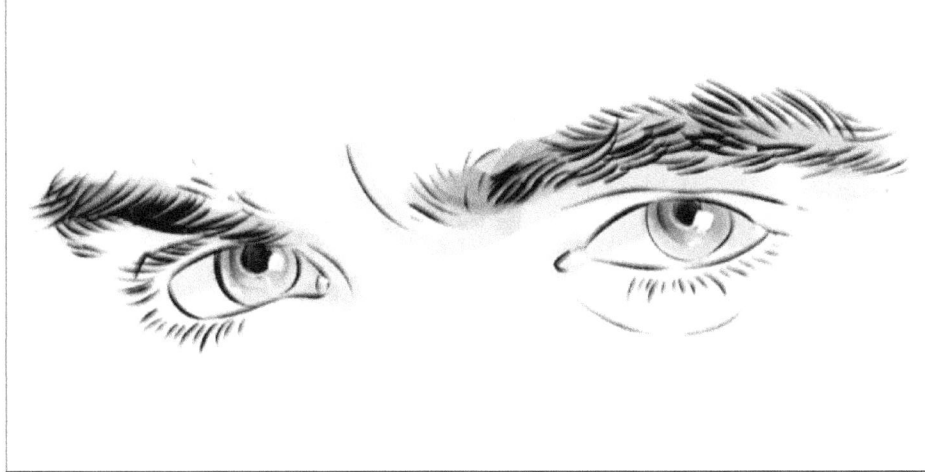

Eyes 4- revengeful eyes (male)

When a person bends his head a little and looks straight ahead, the eyes give a scornful or revengeful look. This man's eyes are giving the same vindictive look. Notice that there are differences in the shape of left and right eye, which is very common in humans. The eyes of a person can be significantly different to each other. The difference is not visible at a distance, but when you look closely or at portrait photography, you may notice the difference.

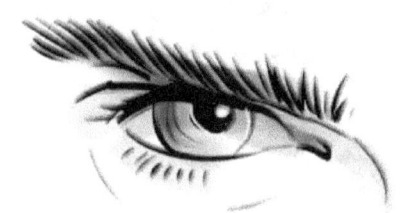 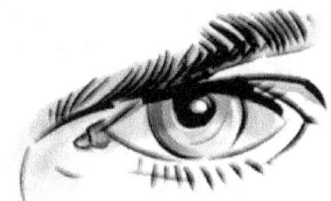

Lips
Gratified lips

These female lips denote gratification with food or something else. Lips are the second most expressive feature after eyes. That is why; you need to draw the lips and teeth with precision. The lips also consist of many fine lines, which contribute to the quality of your drawing. While drawing teeth, you must notice that teeth are never flat white in color. Most people have off- white color of teeth. Even if the color of the teeth is consistent, you will definitely notice shadow of lips on the teeth.

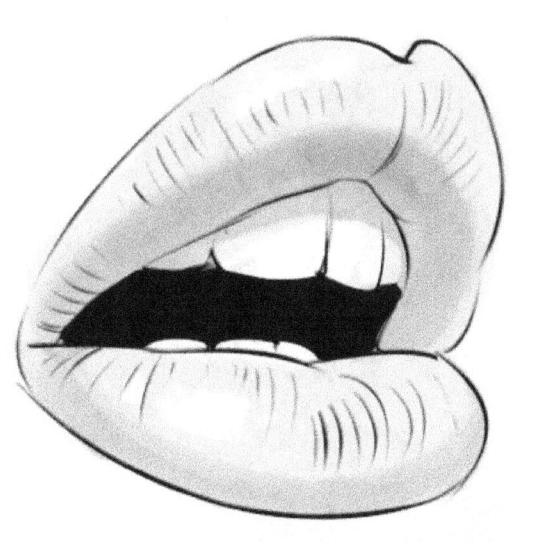

Lips 2- lusty lips

These lips also belong to a female. She has slightly tucked her lips with her teeth, which gives a lusty look to her lips. Notice that there are abundant fine lines in her lips, which give rise to different tonal values. Since the lips are tucked with the teeth, the shape of the lips is considerably different from normal.

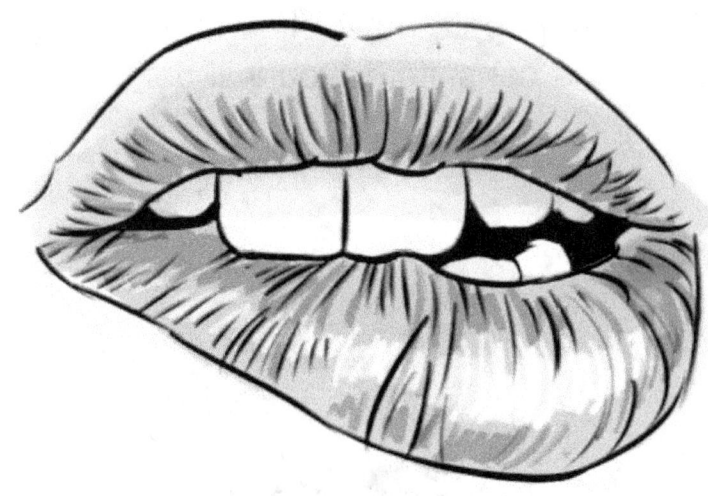

Nose

Nose is very easy to draw because it hardly contributes to expressing emotions in a face.

However, you have to be very careful while drawing a nose. Since nose does not have well defined boundary, you have to give it the required shape just by using gradations for the maximum part. If you are drawing a nose from the side profile, much of your work is reduced because you can give a definite shape to the nose. Only one nostril has to be drawn from the side profile.

Nose 1

This nose is drawn from the side profile. There is a bump in the bridge of the nose, which is depicted by small arcs.

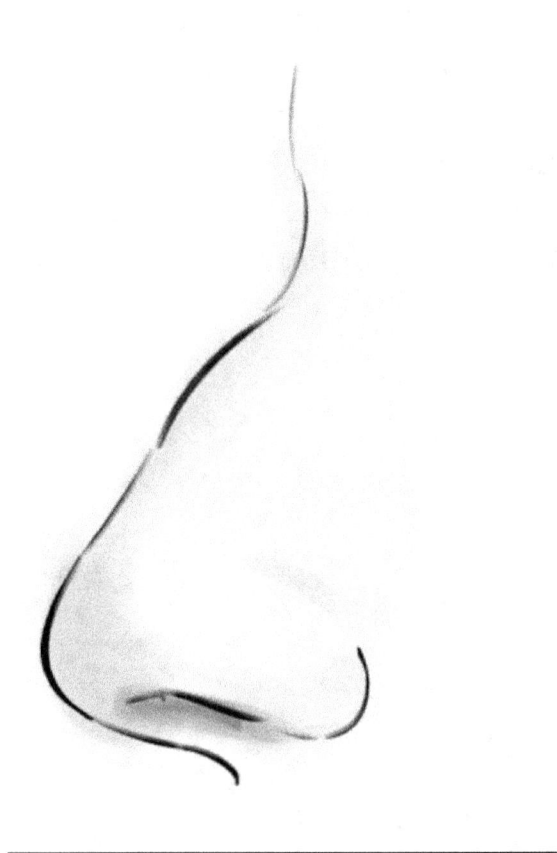

Nose 2

This nose is drawn from the front profile. Notice that there are hardly any lines drawn to depict the bridge of the nose. Only the nostrils and their sides have to be drawn with definite lines.

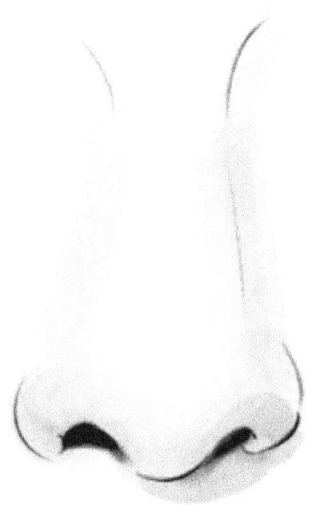

Nose 3

This nose is also drawn from a side profile. Hence, it does not require much effort in drawing.

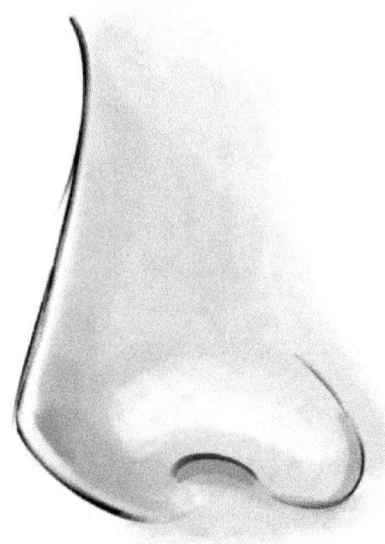

Chapter 3
Portrait of Ana (female)

Step 1

Draw the basic outline of Ana from the side profile. The lady is sitting straight but her face is turned sideways.

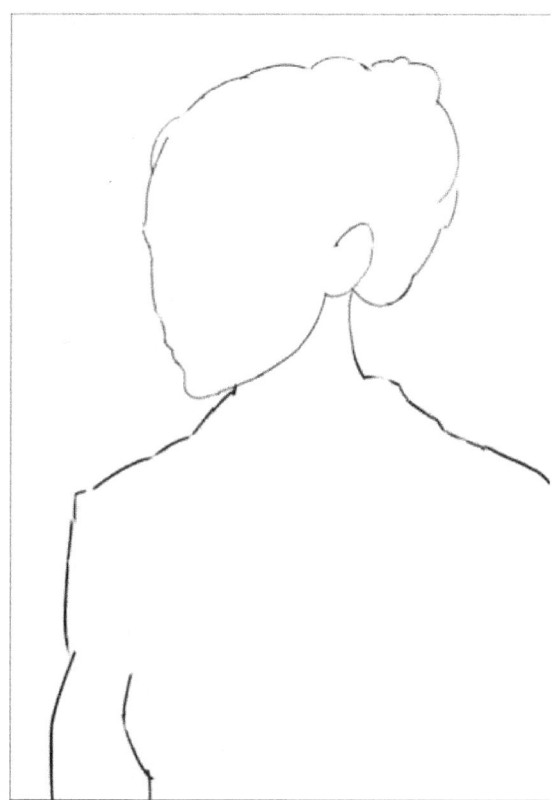

Step 2

Draw the lines to place eyes, nose, and lips. Notice that her right ear falls between the eyes and nose. Draw her clothing as she is wearing a collared shirt.

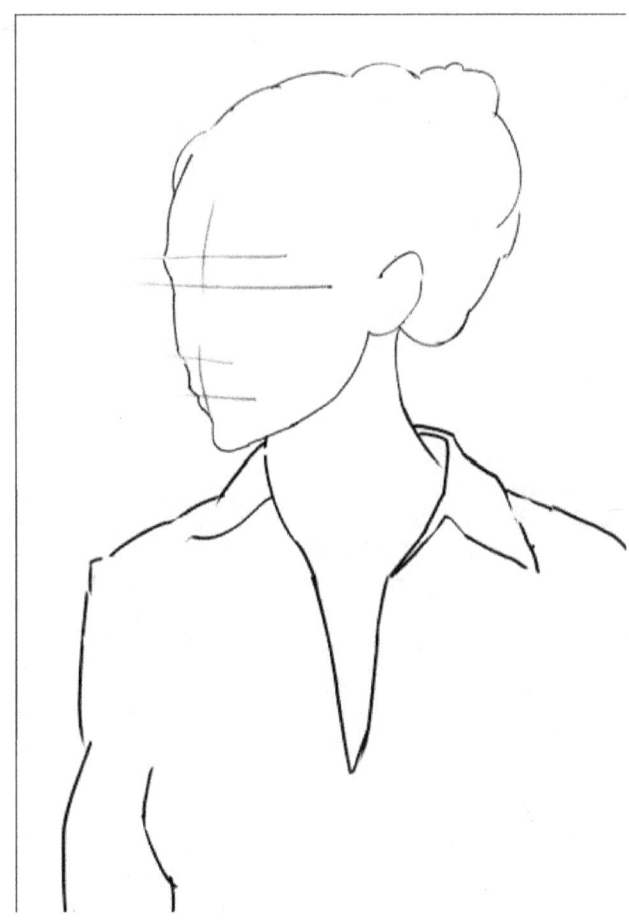

Step 3

Draw the eyes, nose, lips, and ears with slight details. The left eye and lips are not completely visible since Ana is looking sideways.

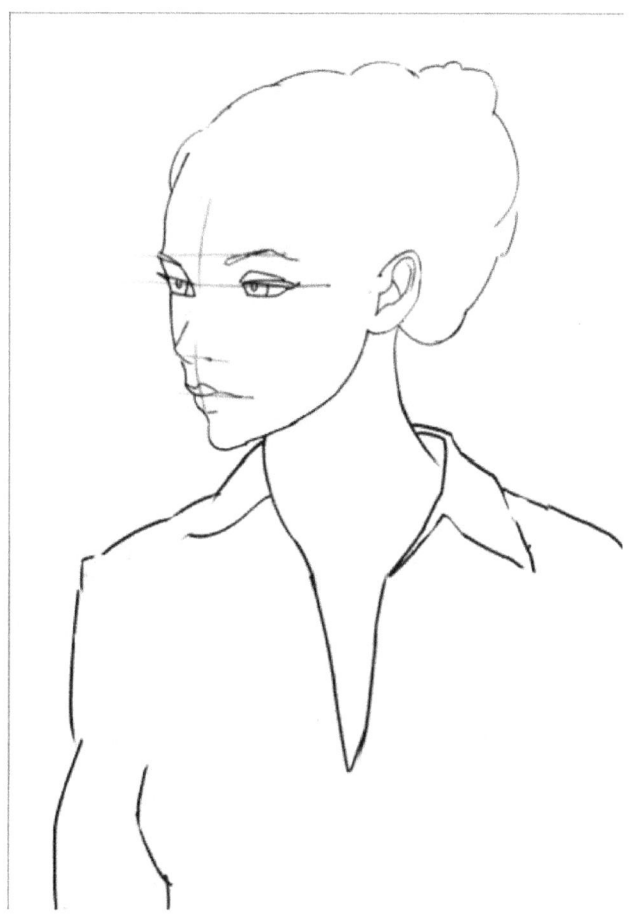

Step 4

Draw strokes to depict strands of her hairs. The hairs never fall in the same direction. Therefore, draw the strands in different directions.

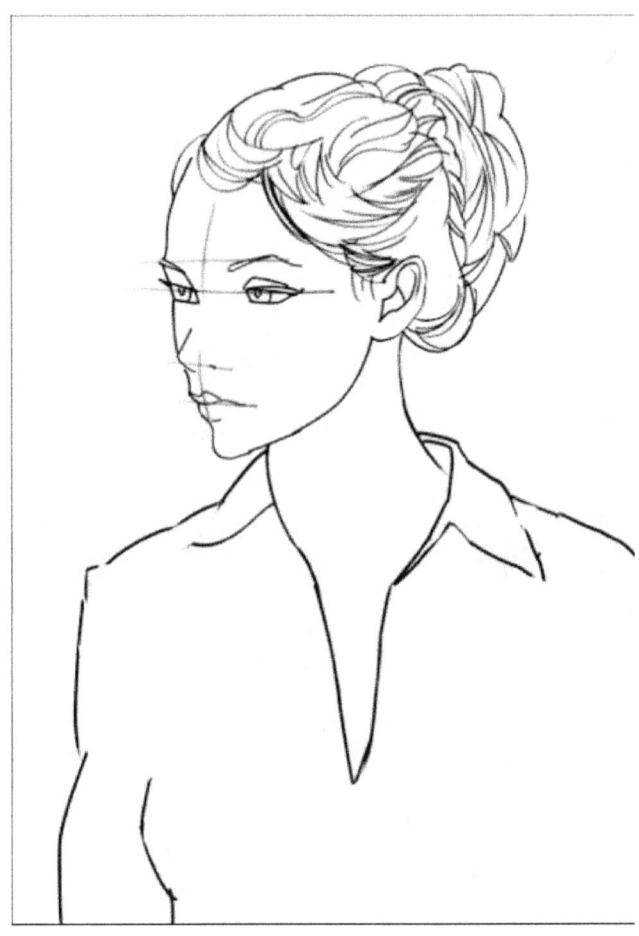

Step 5

Draw the buttons of her shirt and the pockets. Notice the creases on her clothing. These details are crucial to characterize a portrait.

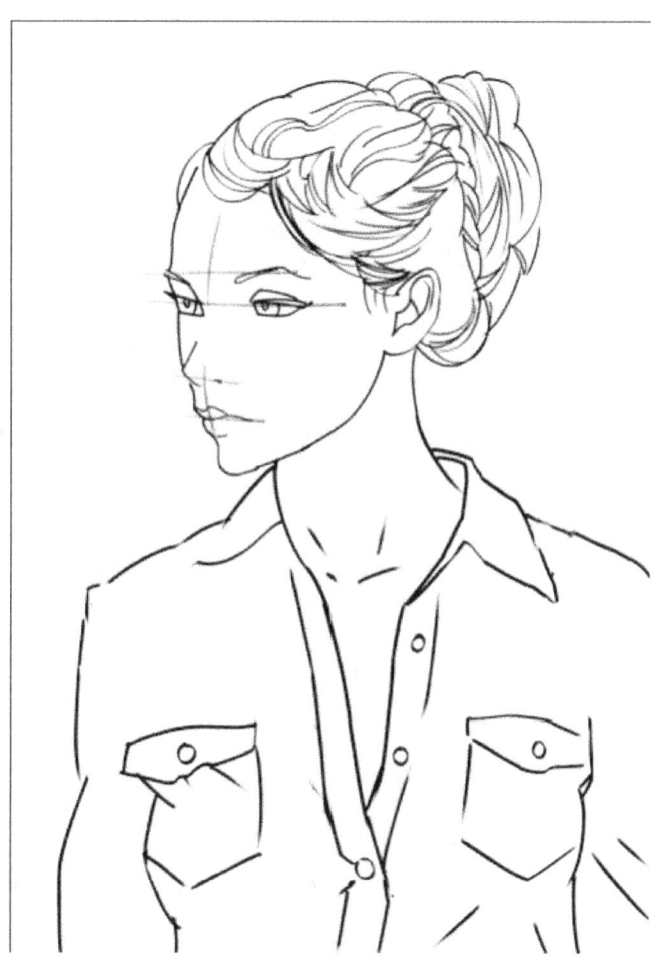

Step 6

Draw a few more creases in her shirt.

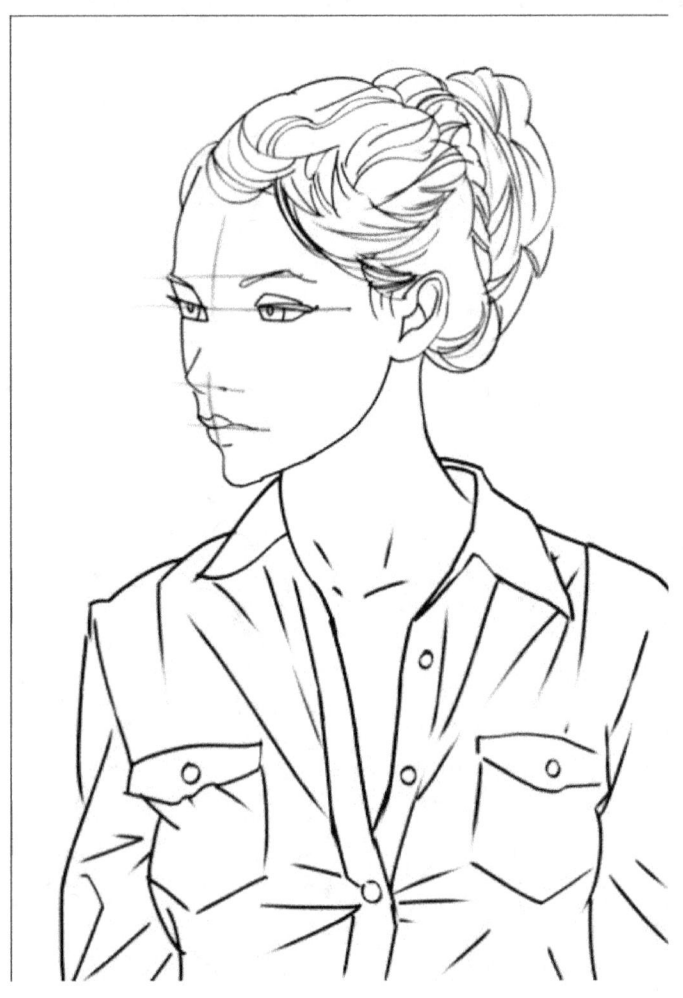

Step 7

Erase the lines from the face that were used to place the features. Since these vertical and horizontal lines have to be erased later, you must draw them with lighter shade of pencil.

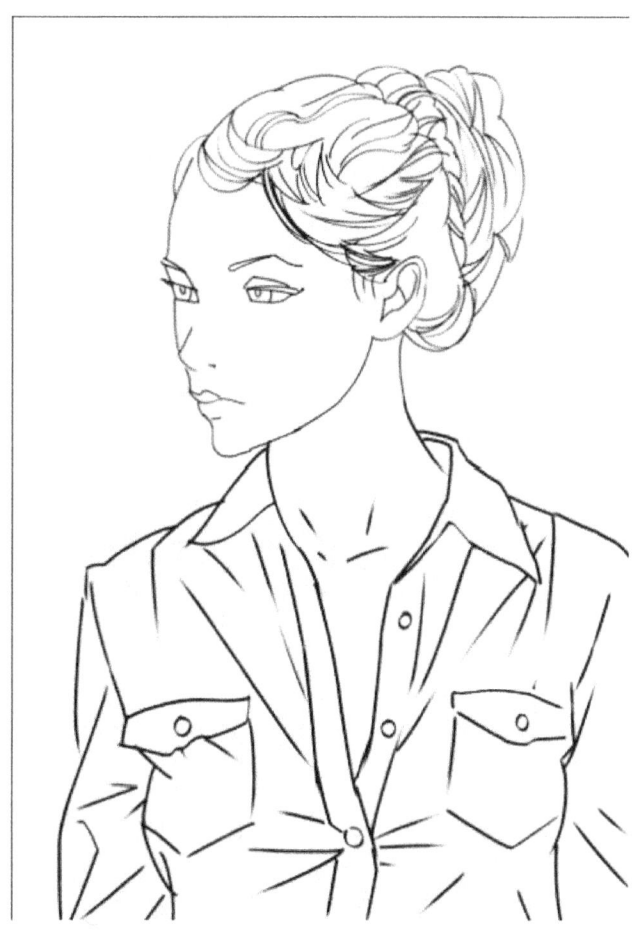

Step 8

Now, start giving shading slightly in different parts of the portrait of Ana.

Give shading in her eyes and most part of her shirt.

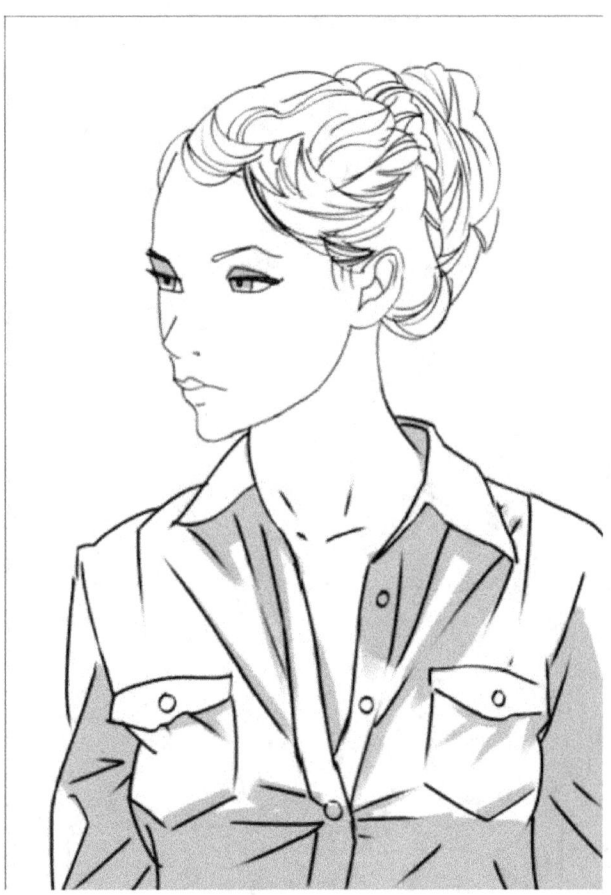

Step 9

Give shading in her hairs, face, and neck. The portrait of Ana is complete.

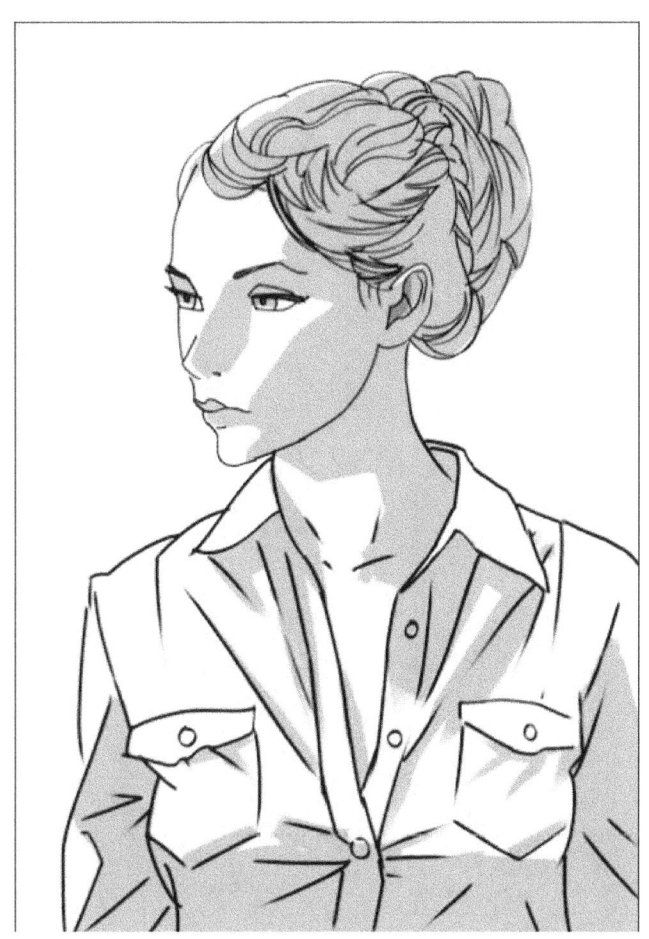

Chapter 4
Portrait of Christy (female)

Step 1

Draw the basic outline of the face of Christy. Draw the vertical and horizontal lines to place the facial features such as eyes, nose, and lips.

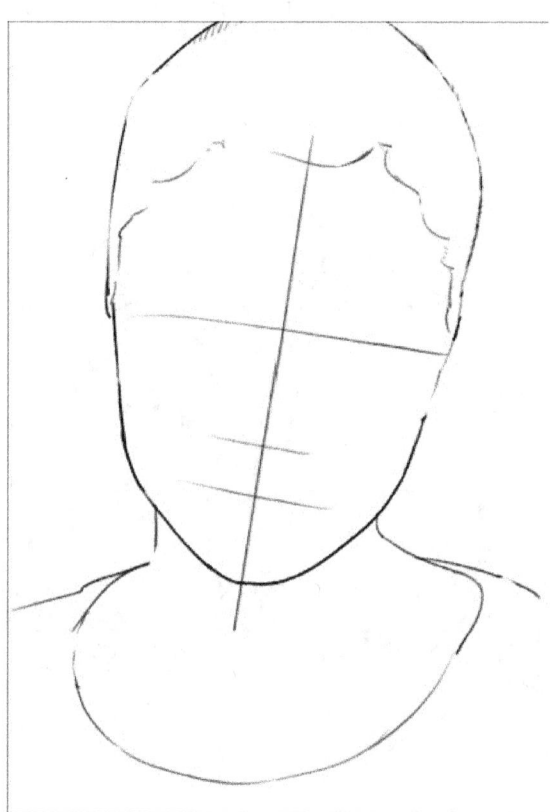

Step 2

Draw her ears and hairs. Since Christy has tied her hair at the back of her head, you do not have to draw the strands in different directions. The strands are pulled back in more or less same direction. Only a few curls of the hairs are visible.

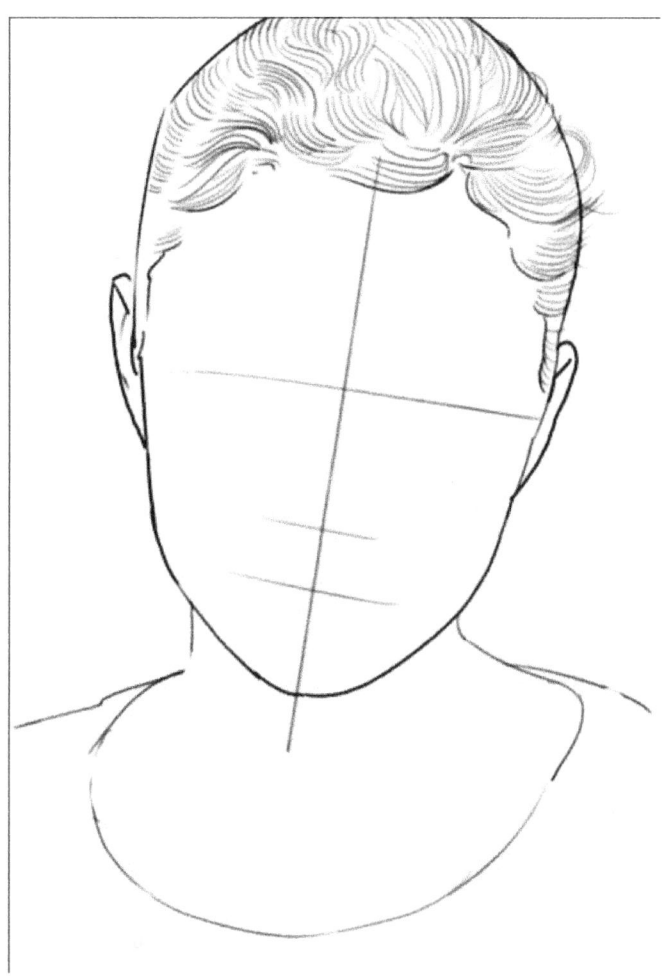

Step 3

Give details to the clothing of Christy. She is wearing a round neck T-shirt and hence, her beauty bones are visible.

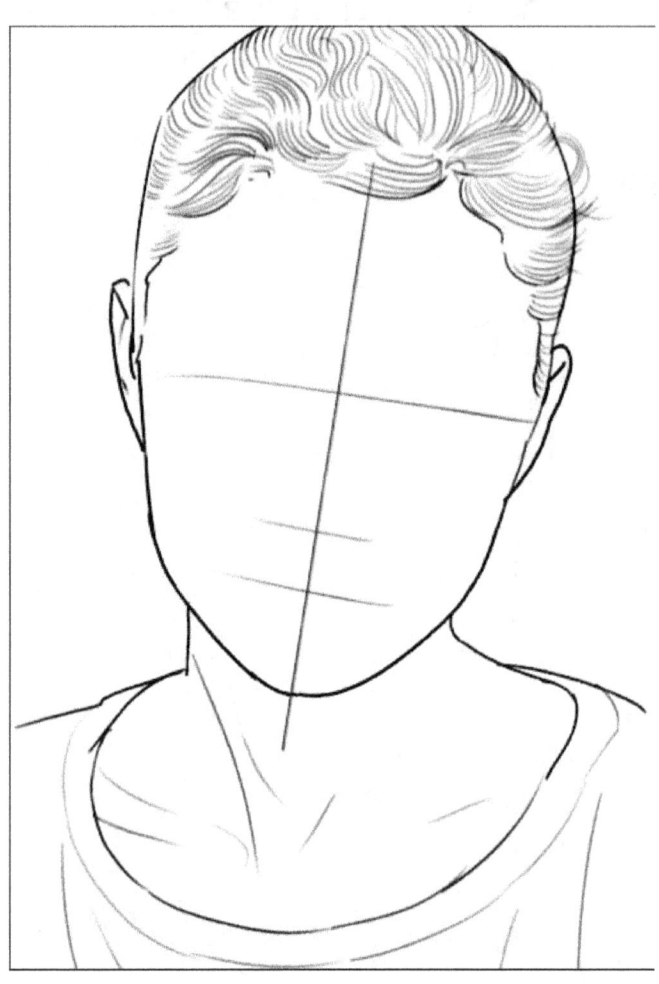

Step 4

Draw the eyes, eyebrows, nose, and lips of the woman. Since she is looking straight at you, you can clearly define her features.

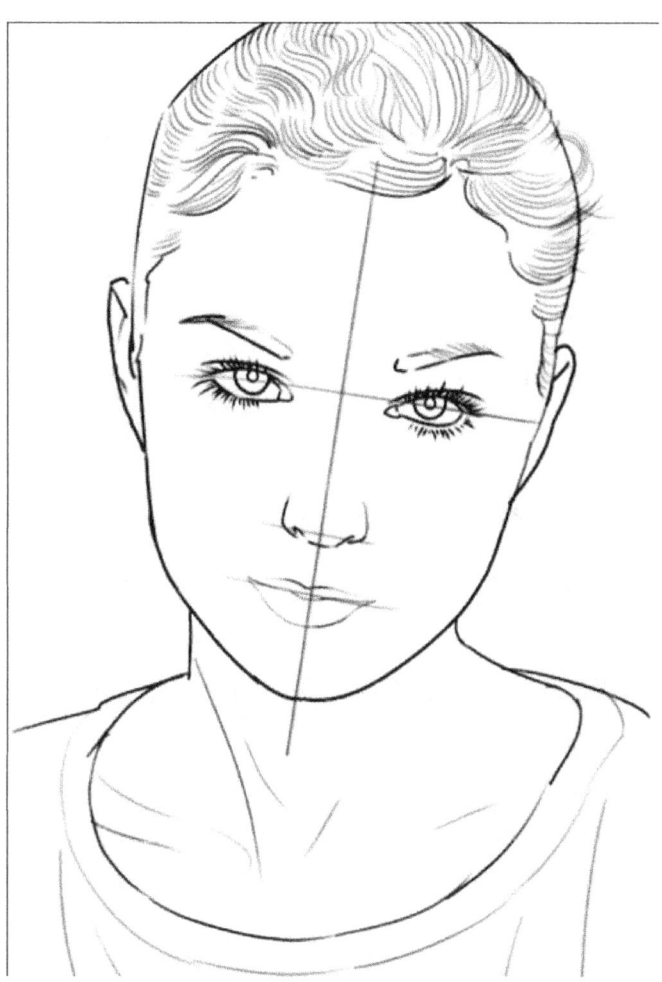

Step 5

Remove the vertical and horizontal lines that were meant for the placement of facial features.

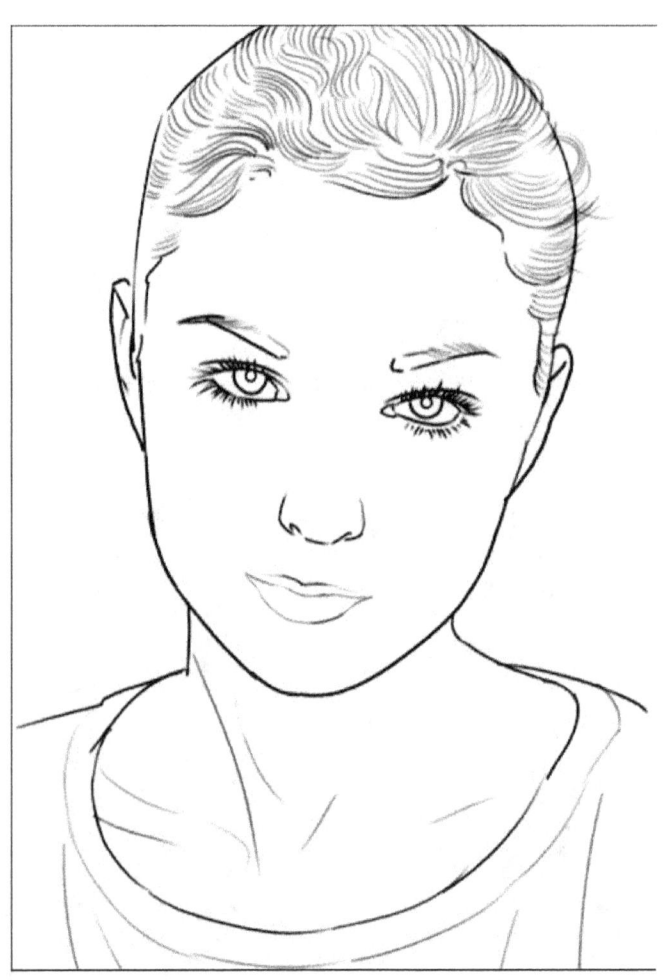

Step 6

Start giving shading in her hairs. Begin with a lighter layer of charcoal shading.

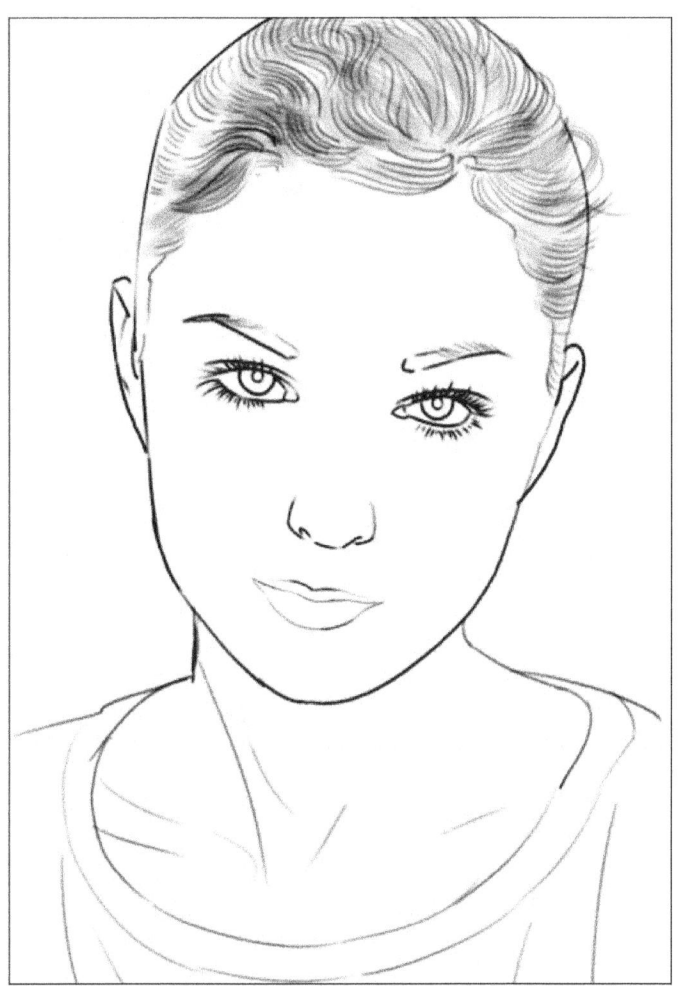

Step 7

Now, give darker shading in some areas of the hairs.

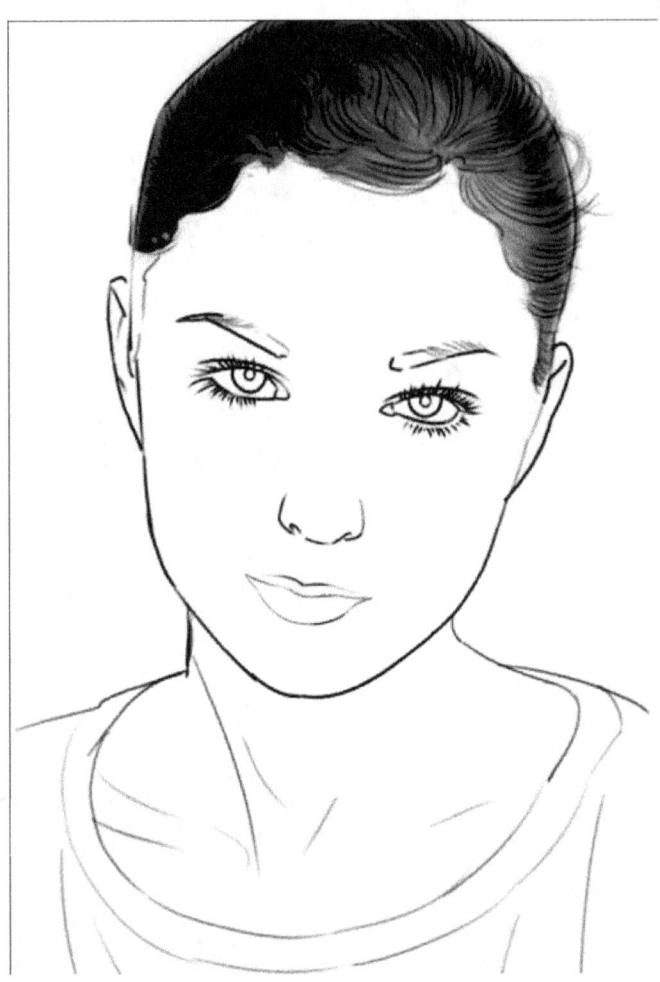

Step 8

Give shading in her eyes, eyebrows, and lips.

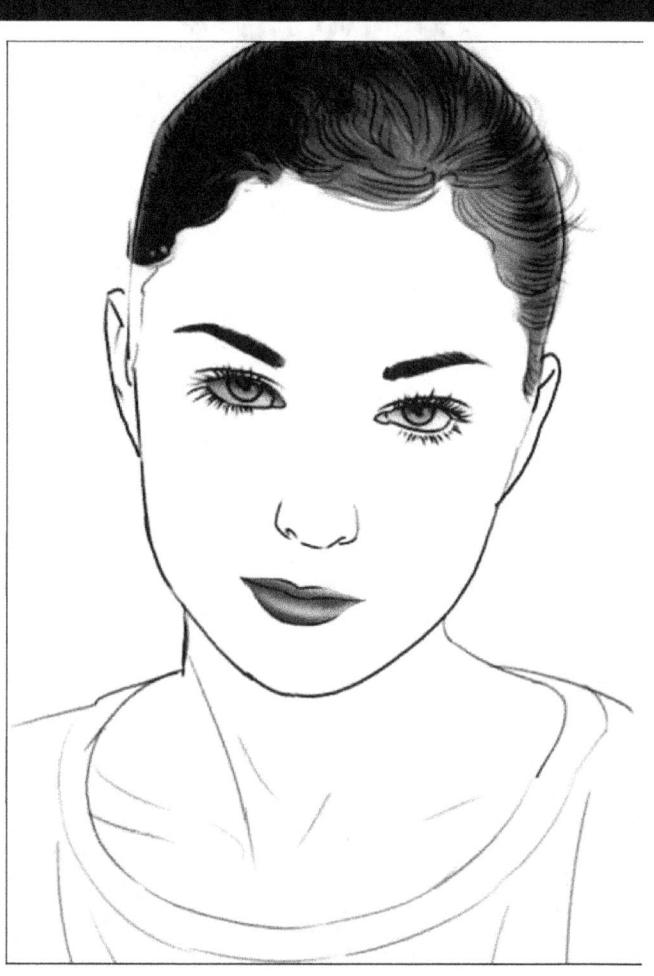

Step 9

Give shading in her clothing.

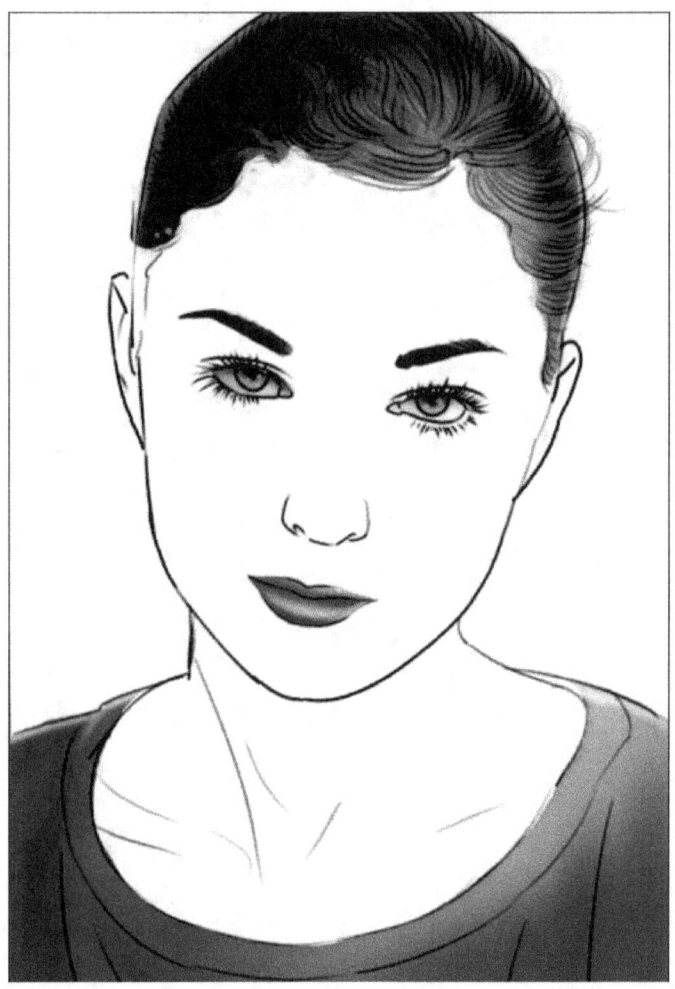

Step 10

Give shading in the neck of Christy.

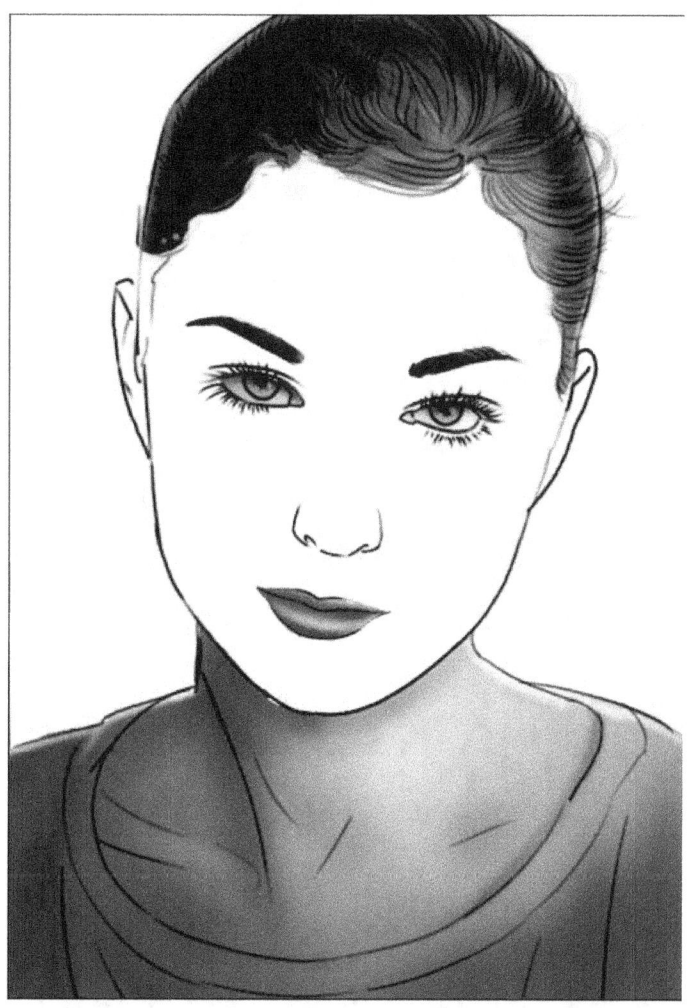

Step 11

Give shading with gradations in her face. Notice that there are darker and lighter portions in the face wherever there are bulges and other changes in the shape of face.

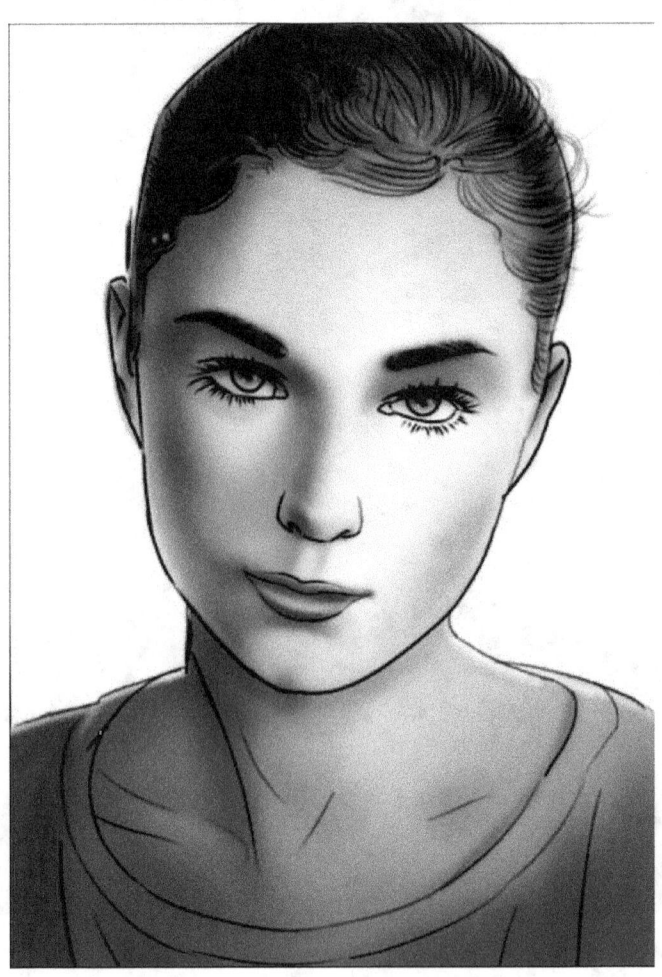

Step 12

To enhance the look of the portrait, give a flat black background in the illustration.

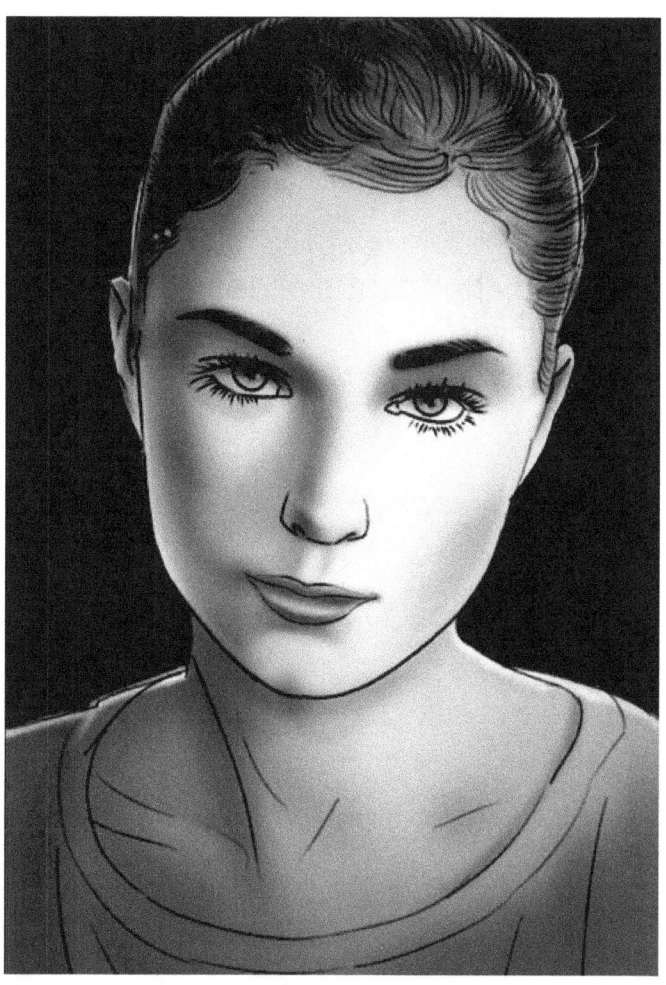

Chapter 5
Portrait of Francesca (female)

Step 1

Draw the basic outline of the face of Francesca. She has a unique hairstyle, with longer hairs on the left side and very sleek hairs on the left.

Draw the vertical and horizontal lines that are meant for the placement of facial features.

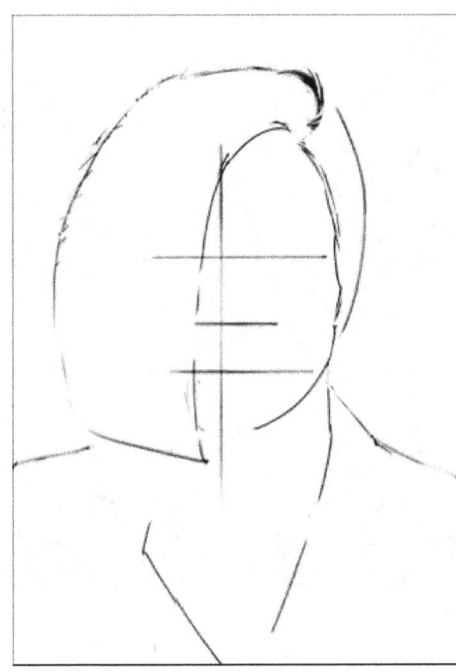

Step 2

Give details of strands of her hairs. The longer hairs are falling on the left side of the face and do not fall in many directions. The shorter hairs on the right side of the face are protruding in different directions.

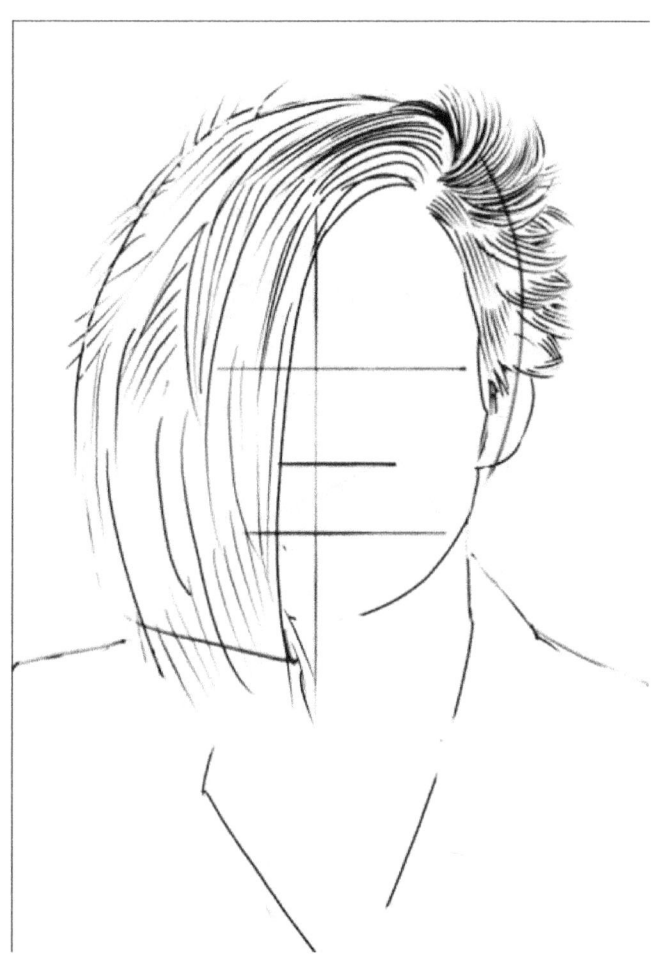

Step 3

Draw the right eye that is visible, and the mouth that displays a few teeth.

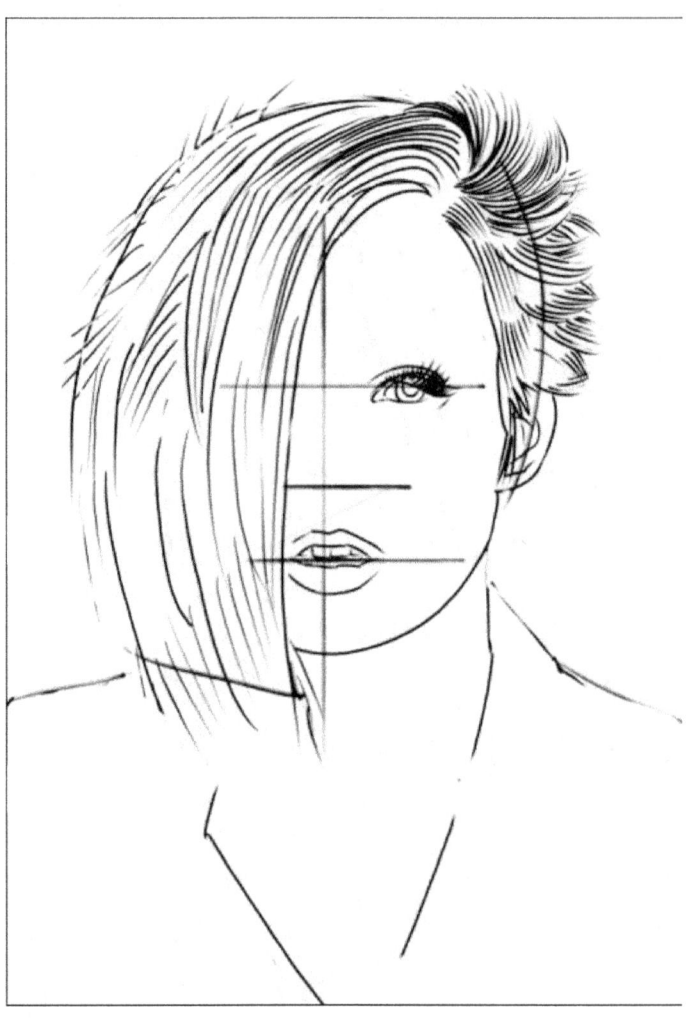

Step 4

Give a few details to her clothing. Francesca has a few rivets placed on her shirt's shoulder.

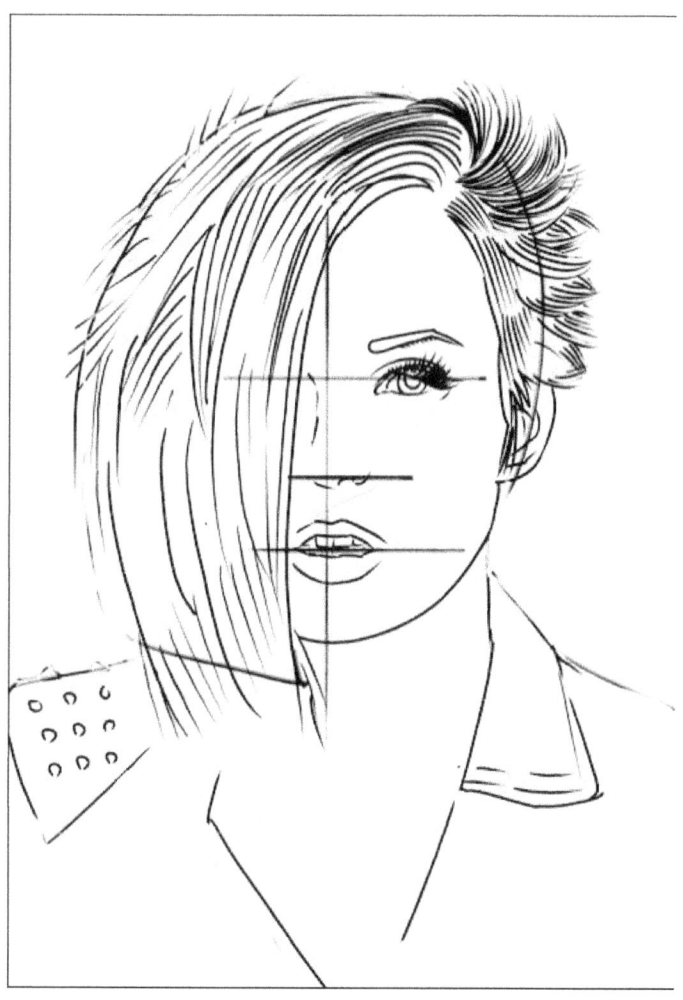

Step 5

Give more details to her clothing as shown in the illustration.

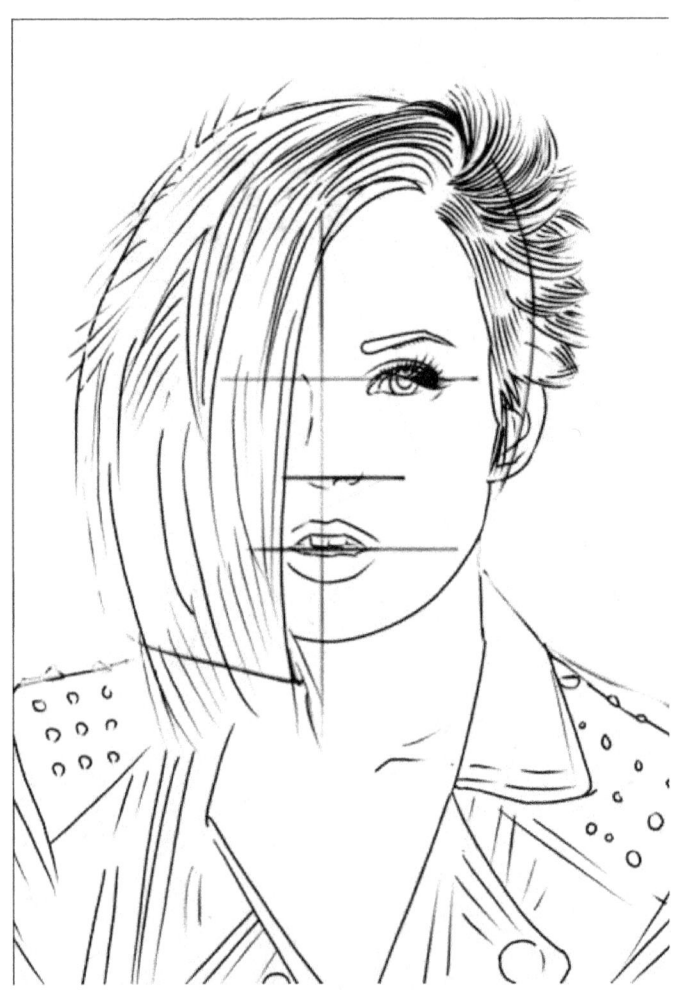

Step 6

Remove the vertical and horizontal lines that were meant for the placement of facial features.

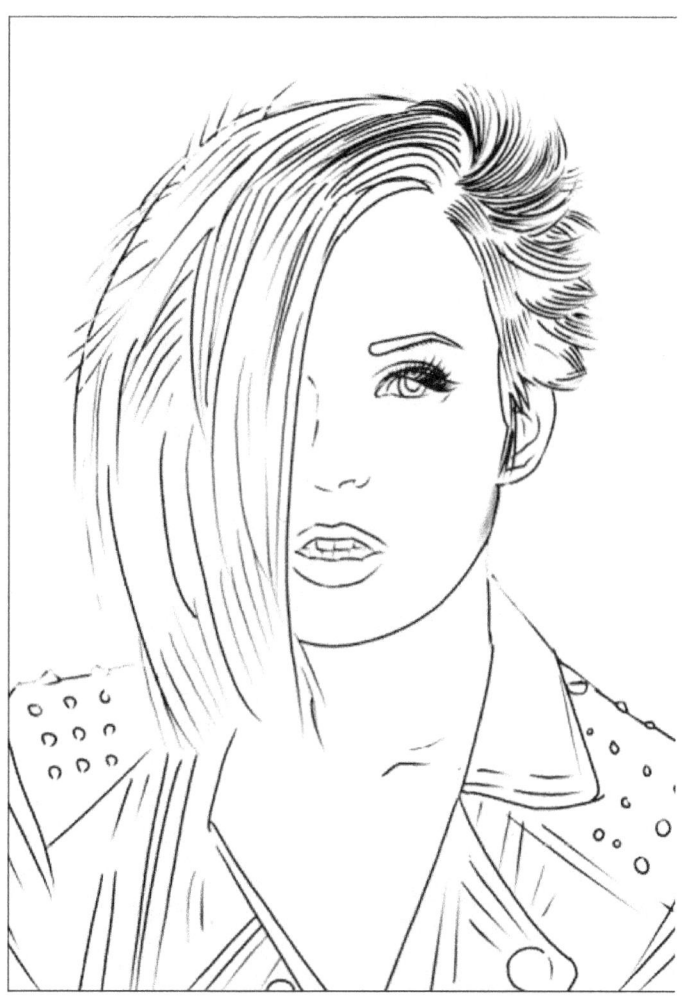

Step 7

Give shading in her face. Notice the gradations in the face because of the tonal values. Give shading in the eyebrow that is visible from her hairs.

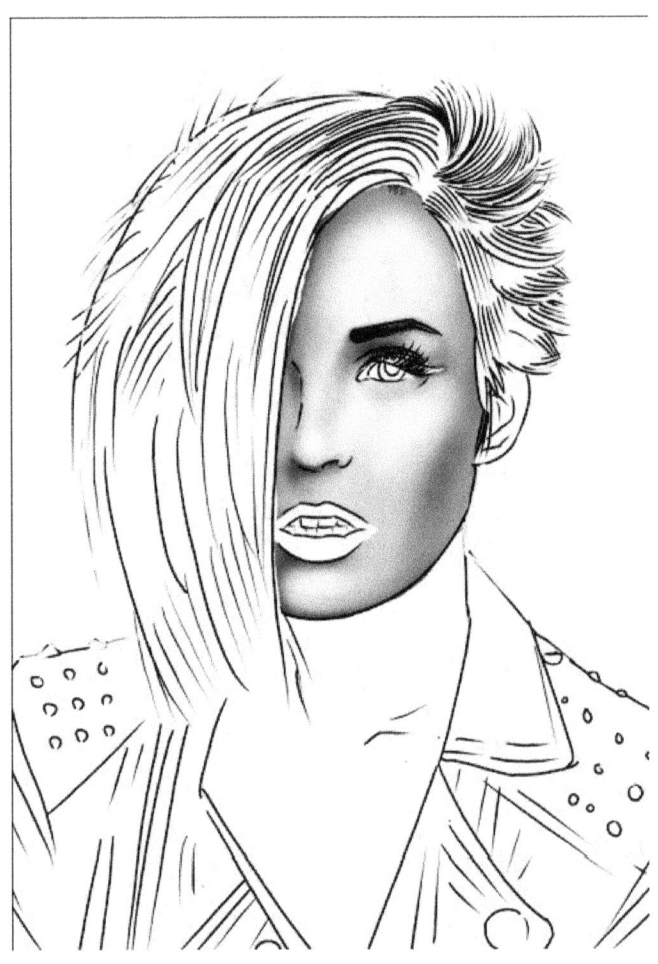

Step 8

Give shading in her eye and enhance her nose.

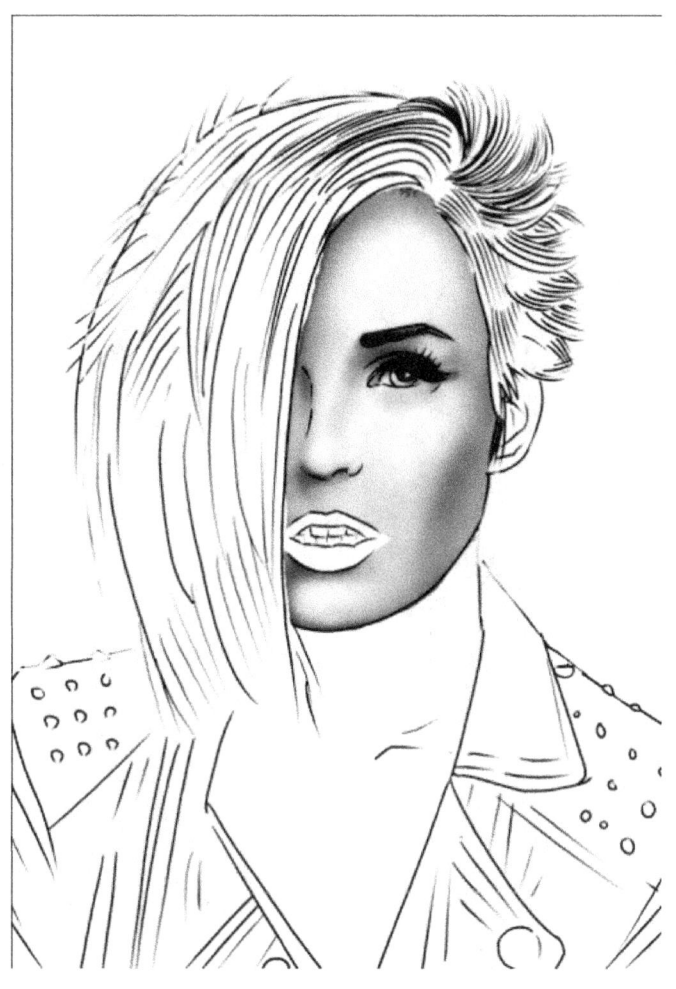

Step 9

Give shading in her hairs.

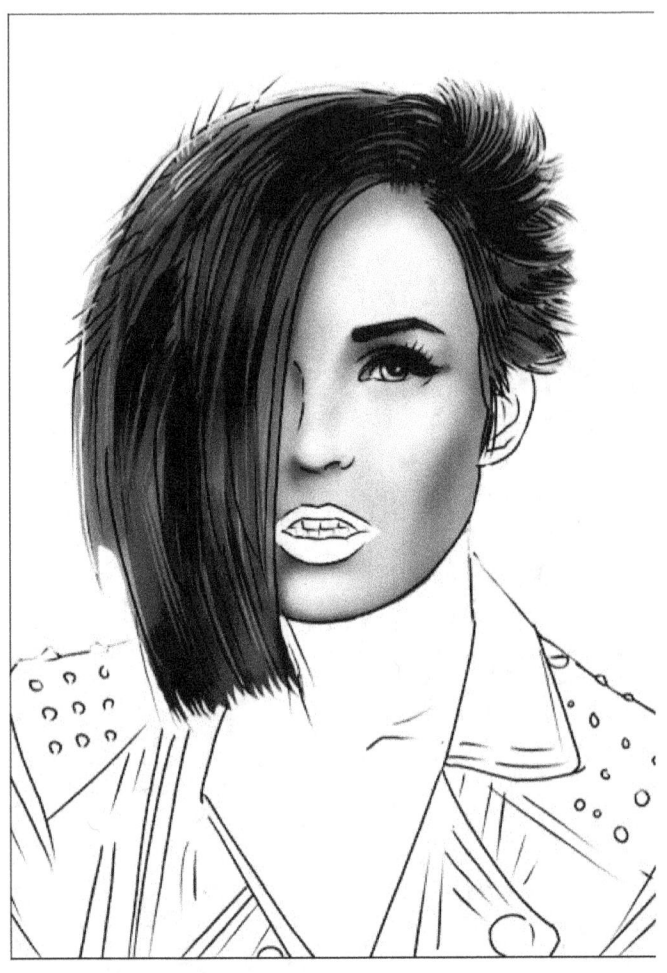

Step 10

Give shading in her neck.

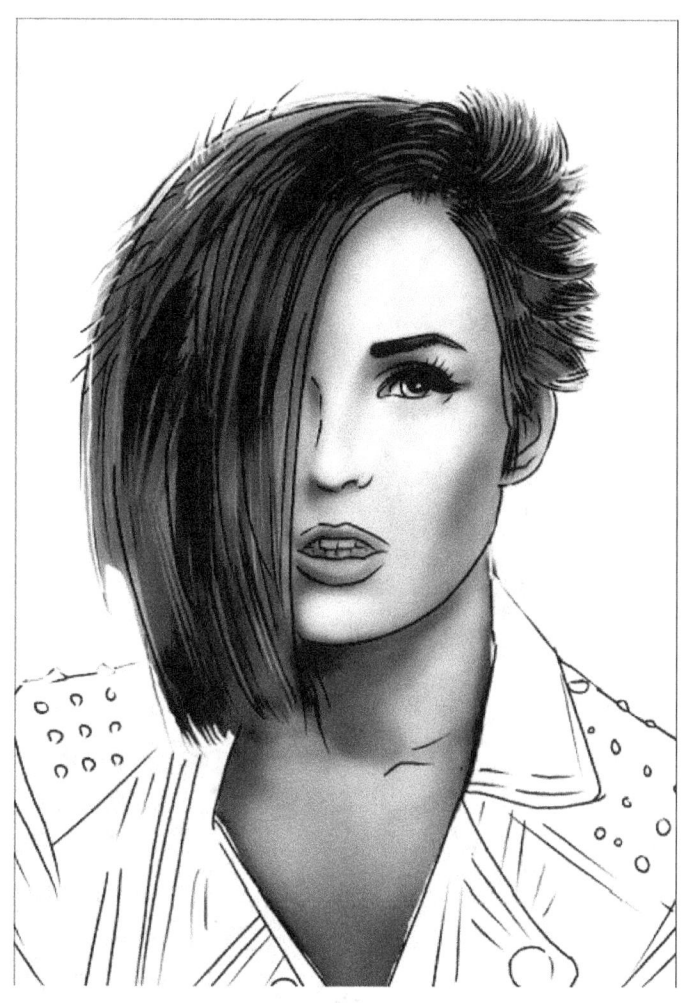

Step 11

Start giving in her clothing. Give shading in the right portion of her shirt.

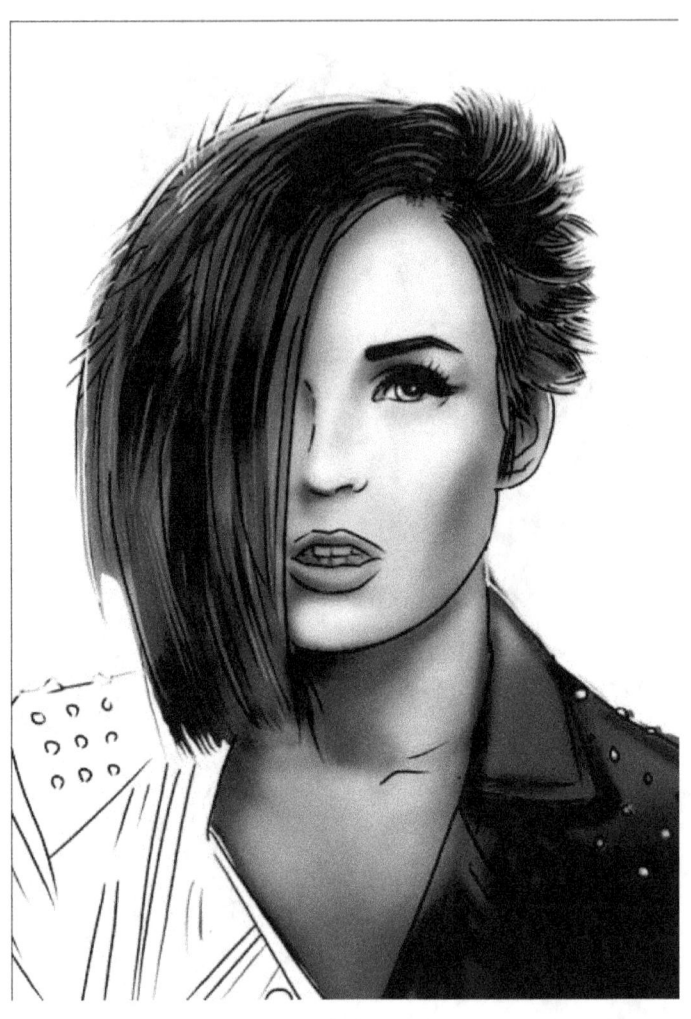

Step 12

Complete the shading in her shirt.

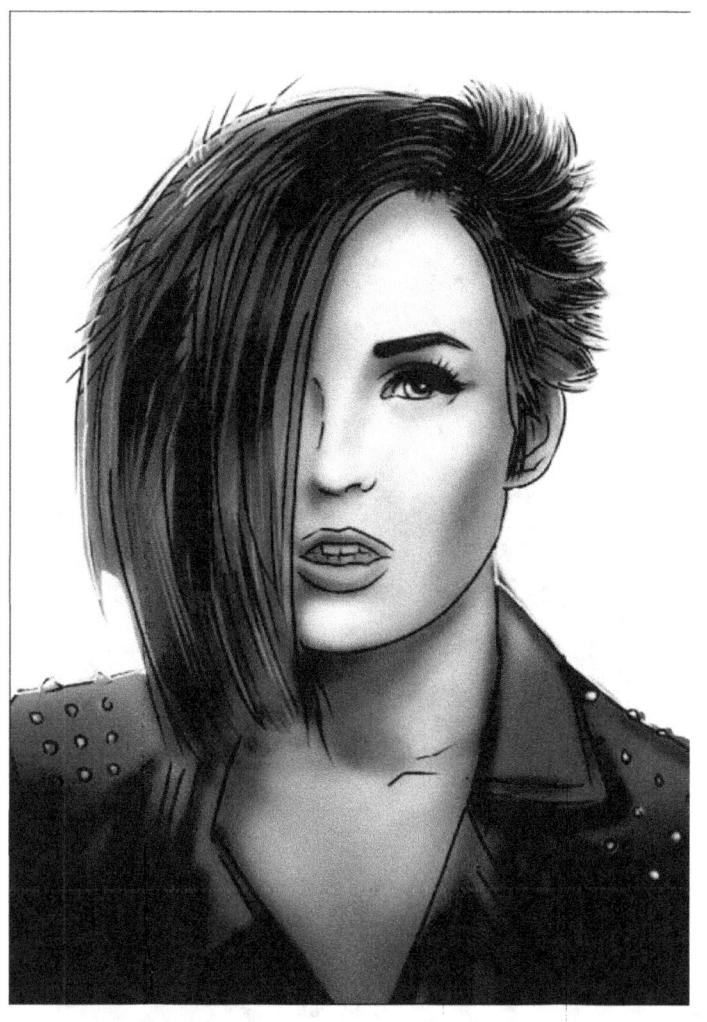

Step 13

To enhance the portrait, give a black background. Give a white reflection on her hairs' edge so that the portrait is not merged with the background.

The portrait of Francesca is ready.

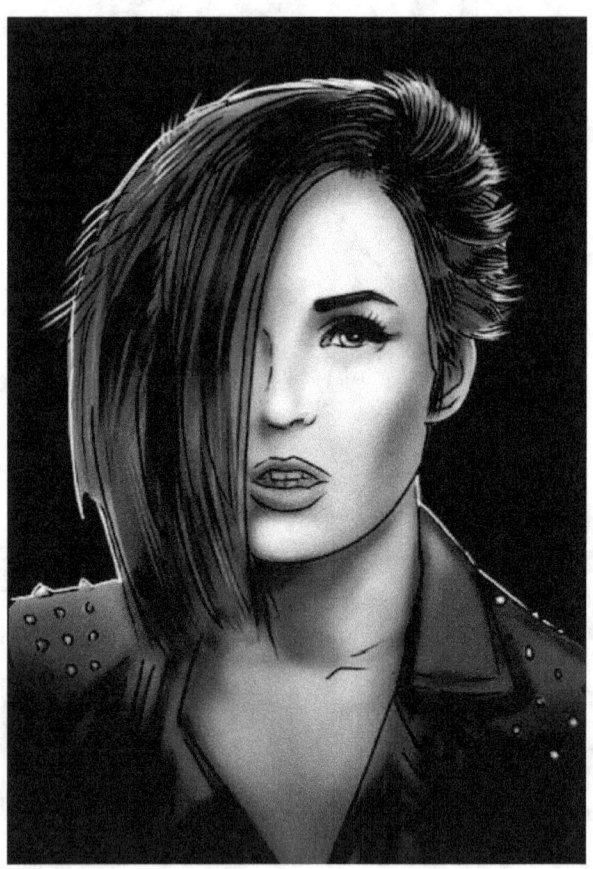

Chapter 6
Portrait of Alexis (male)

Step 1

Draw the basic outline of the face of Alexis. Draw the vertical and horizontal lines that are meant for the placement of facial features.

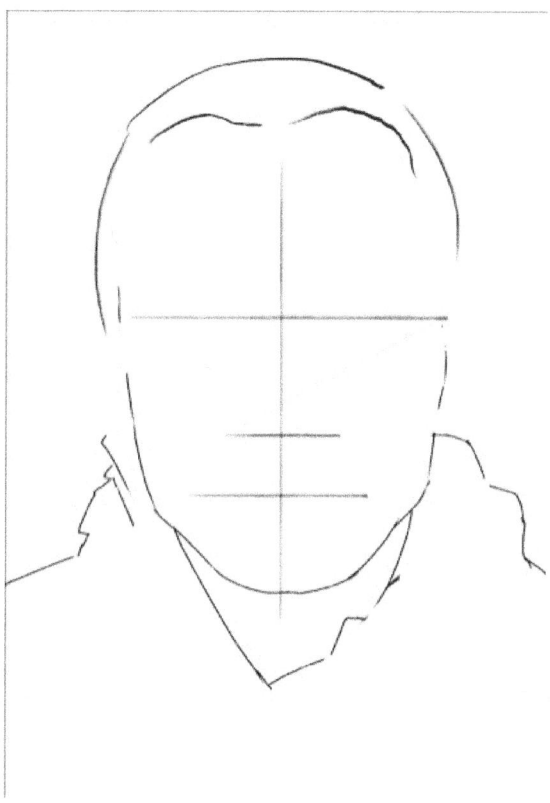

Step 2

Give details of his clothing. He is wearing a high- collared jacket.

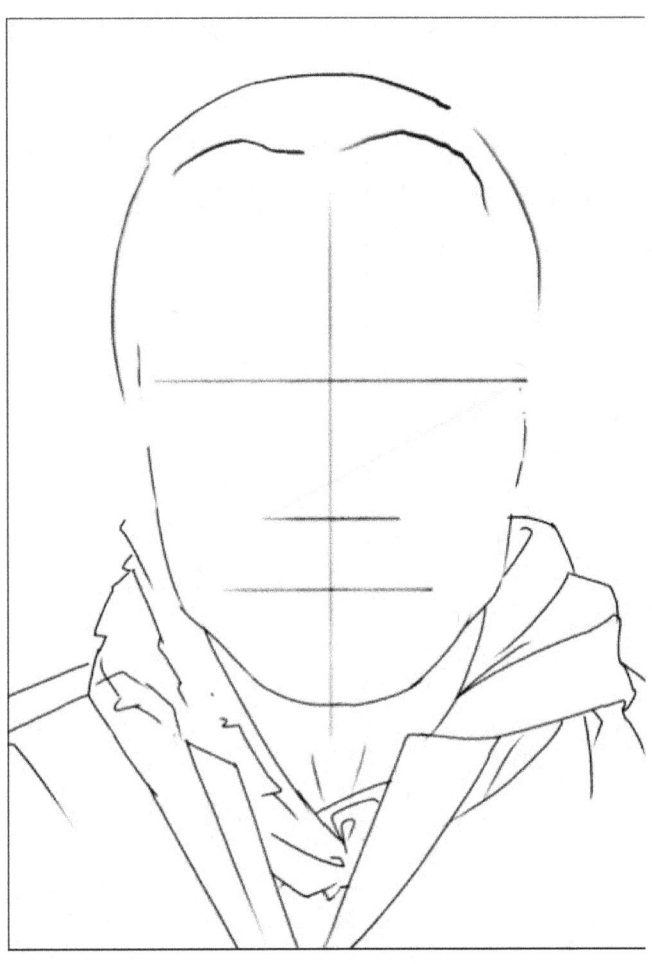

Step 3

Draw the eyebrows of Alexis and some wrinkles on his forehead.

Draw the strands of his hairs. Since his hairs are not very long, you can easily draw his hairs' strands.

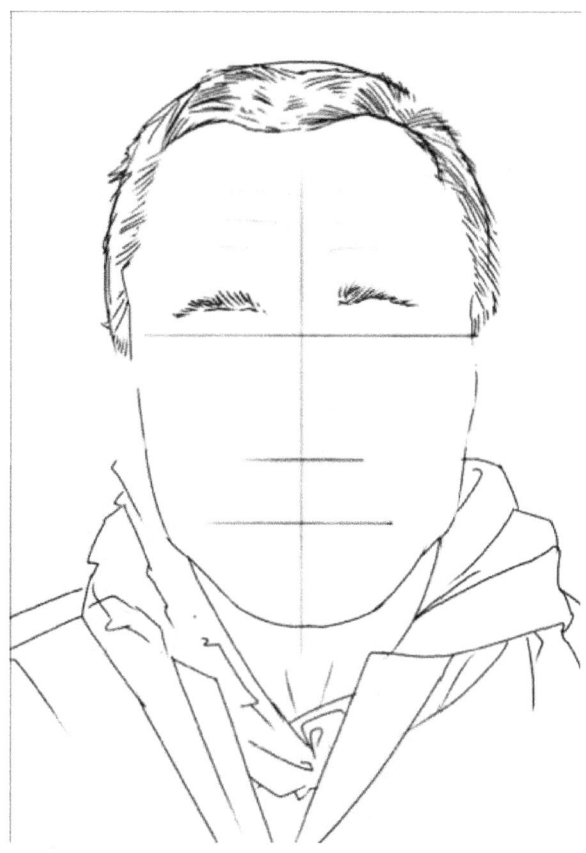

Step 4

Draw his eyes. Since Alexis is a middle- aged man, he has wrinkles on his forehead and his eyes are set a little deep in the eye sockets.

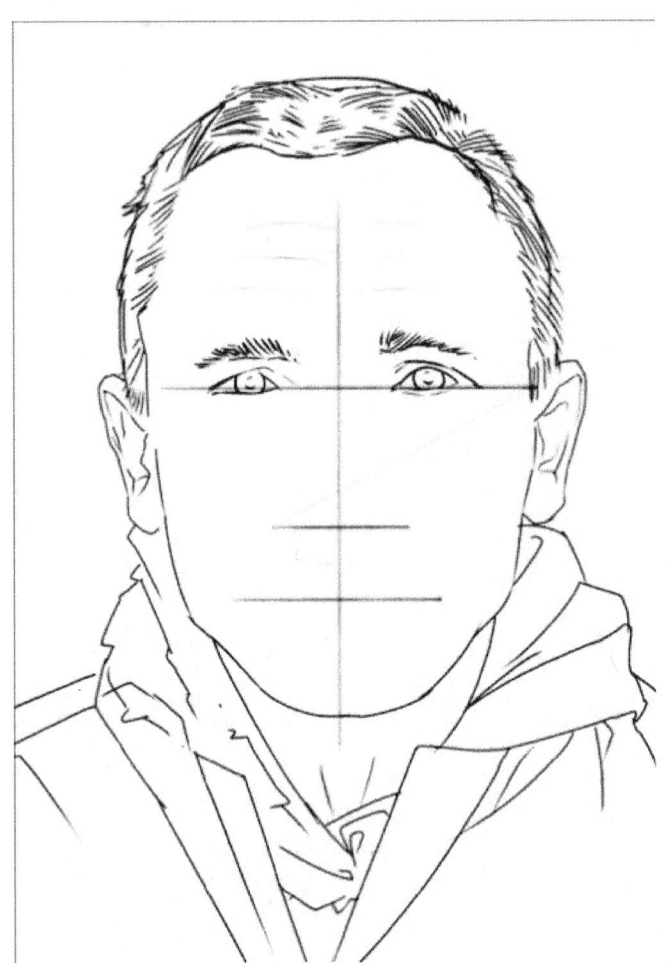

Step 5

Draw his nose and mouth. Notice the lines of his cheek around the nose and mouth, which often occur due to age.

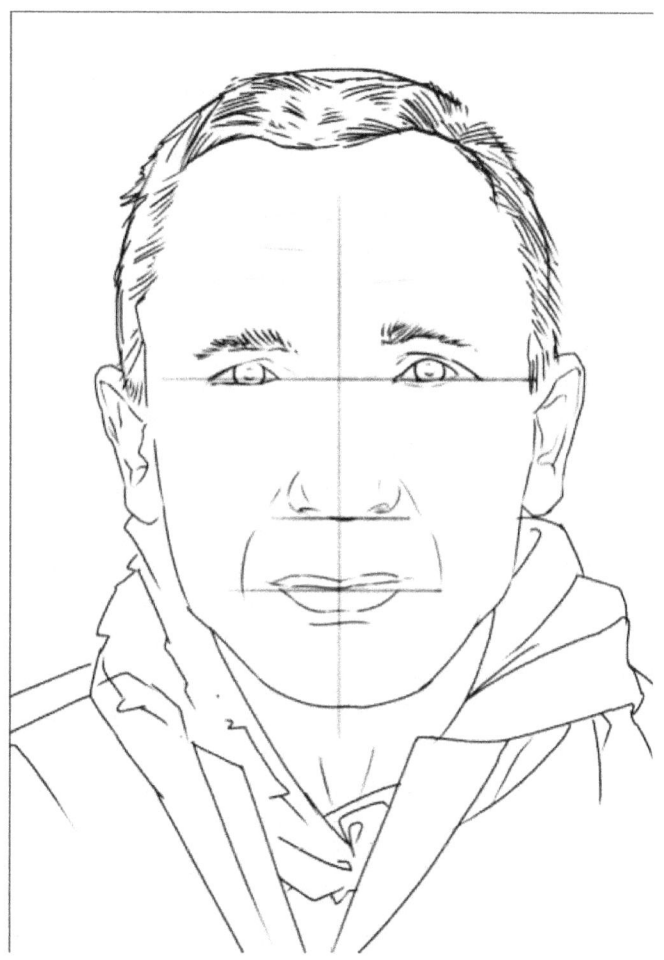

Step 6

Create some wrinkles under his eyes.

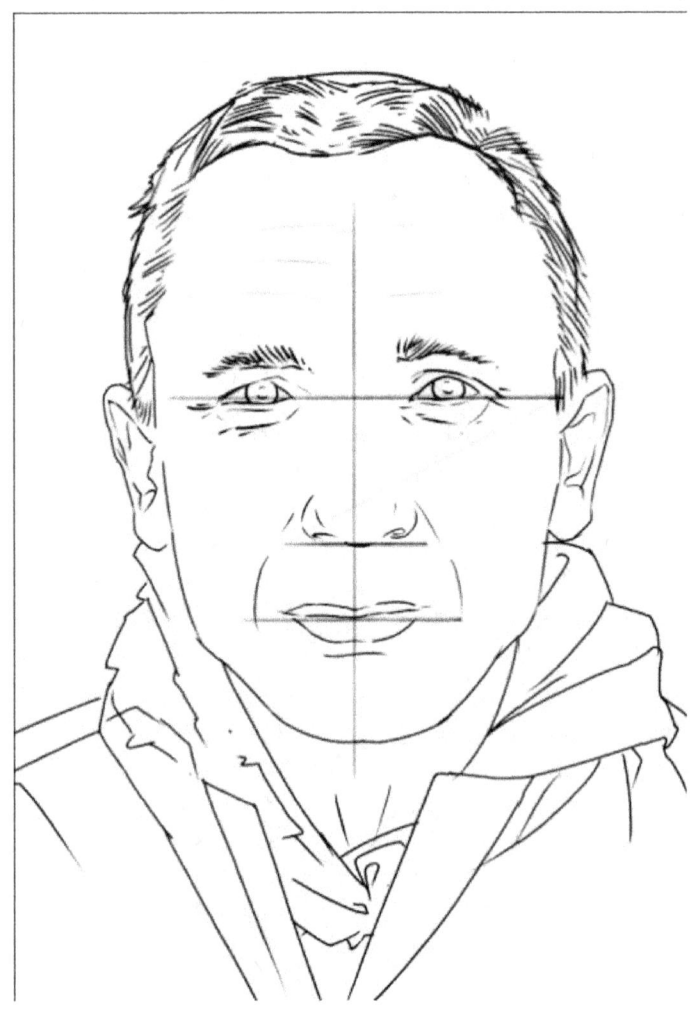

Step 7

Remove the vertical and horizontal lines that were meant for the placement of facial features.

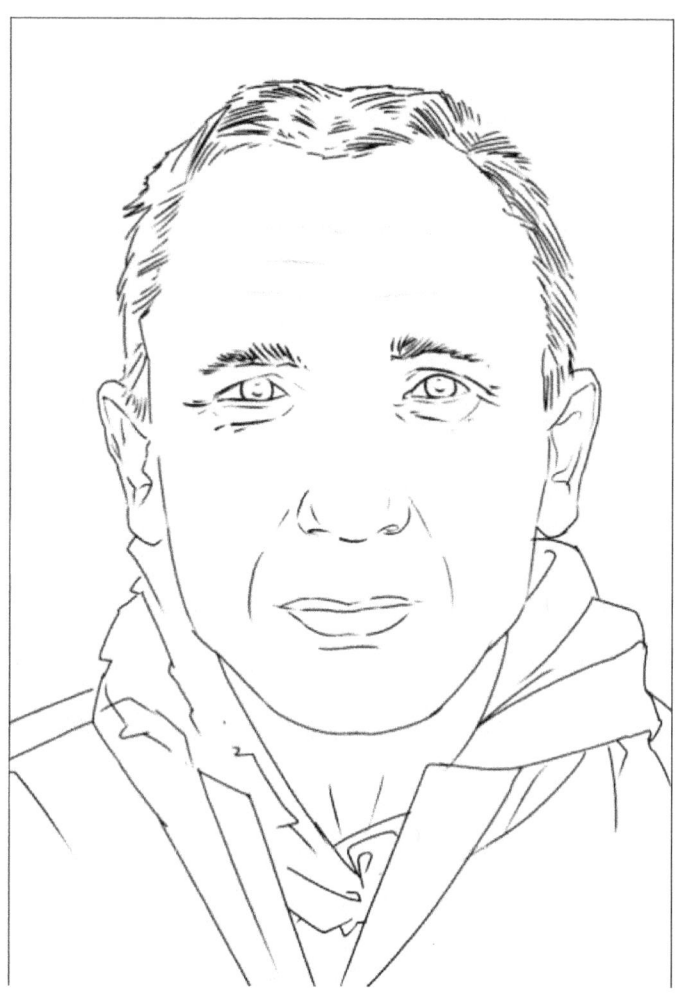

Step 8

Give a light gray background to the portrait.

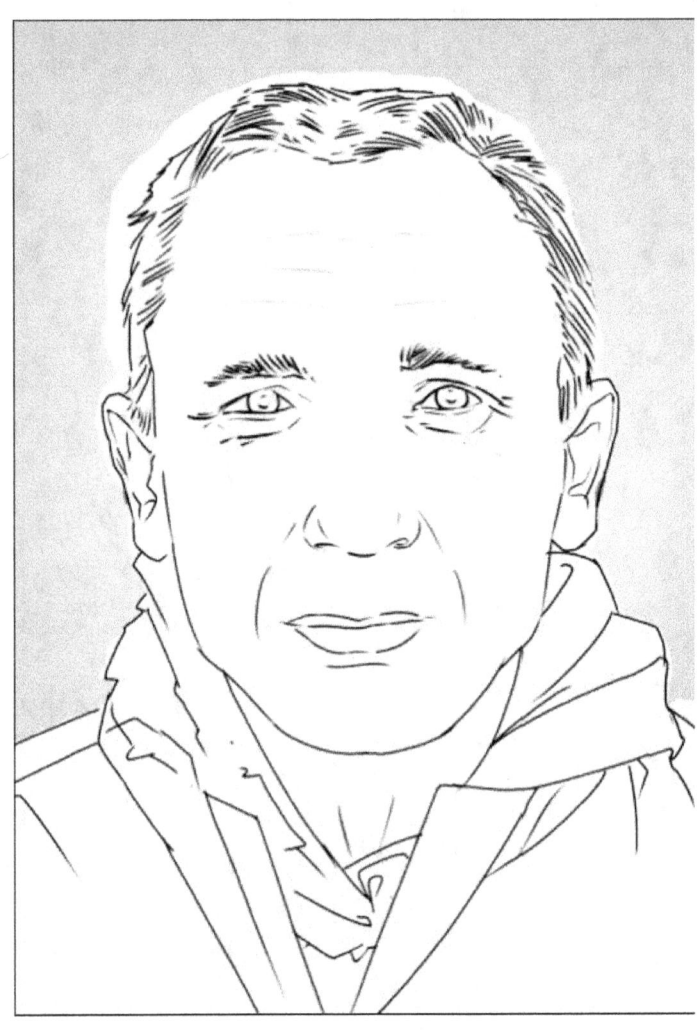

Step 9

Give shading in his face, leaving eyes, nose, and mouth. Notice the changes in shading because of source of light.

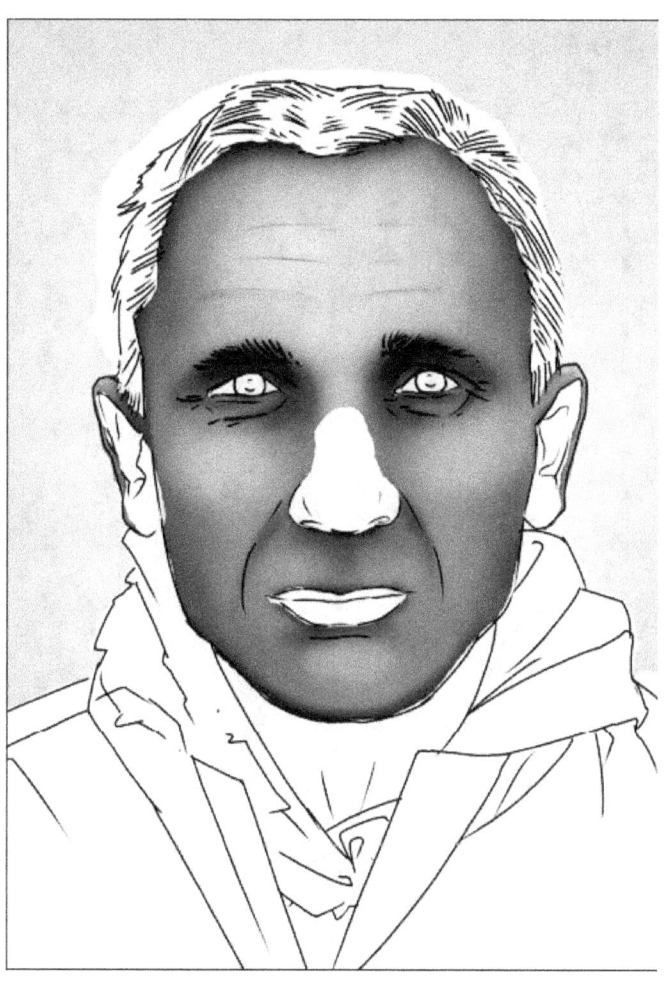

Step 10

Give dark gray shading in his hair, creating to layer of middle tone of gray between the hairs and the background for differentiation.

Give shading in the ears.

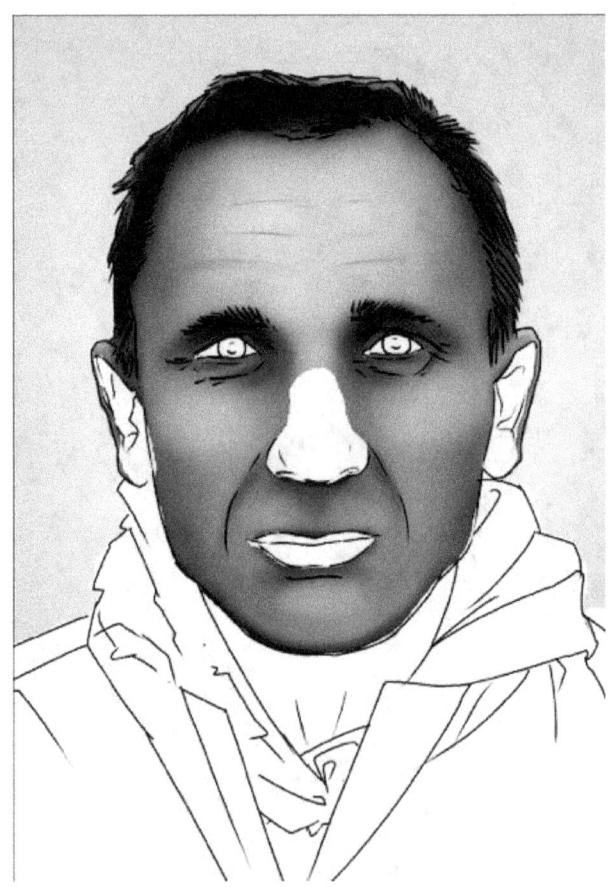

Step 11

Give shading in the lips.

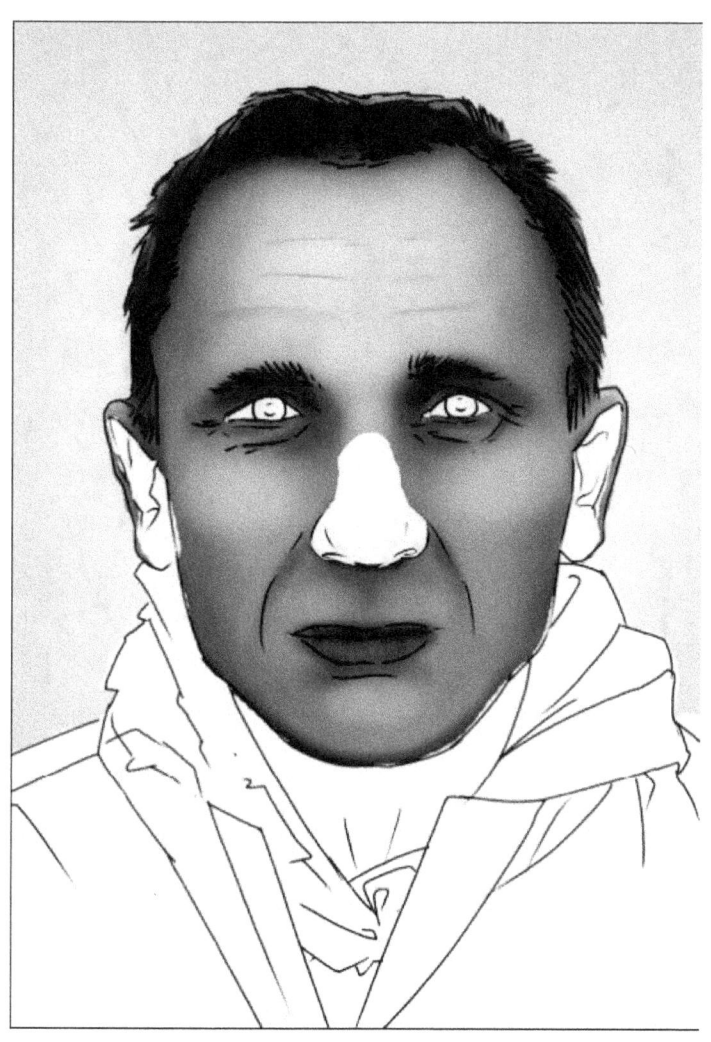

Step 12

Give shading in the eyes and nose.

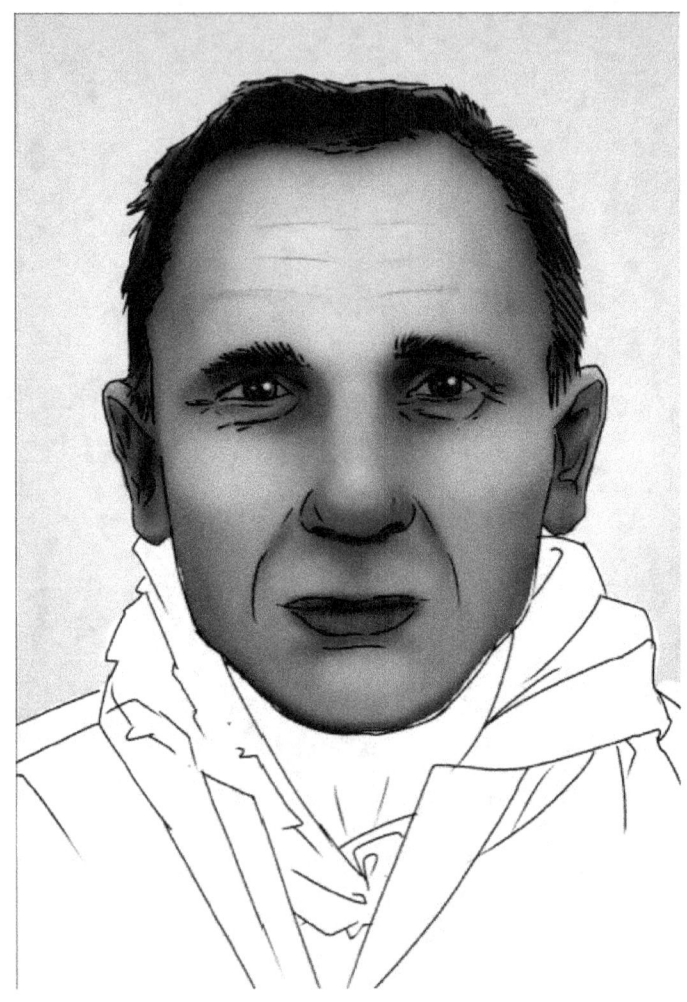

Step 13

Give shading in the neck.

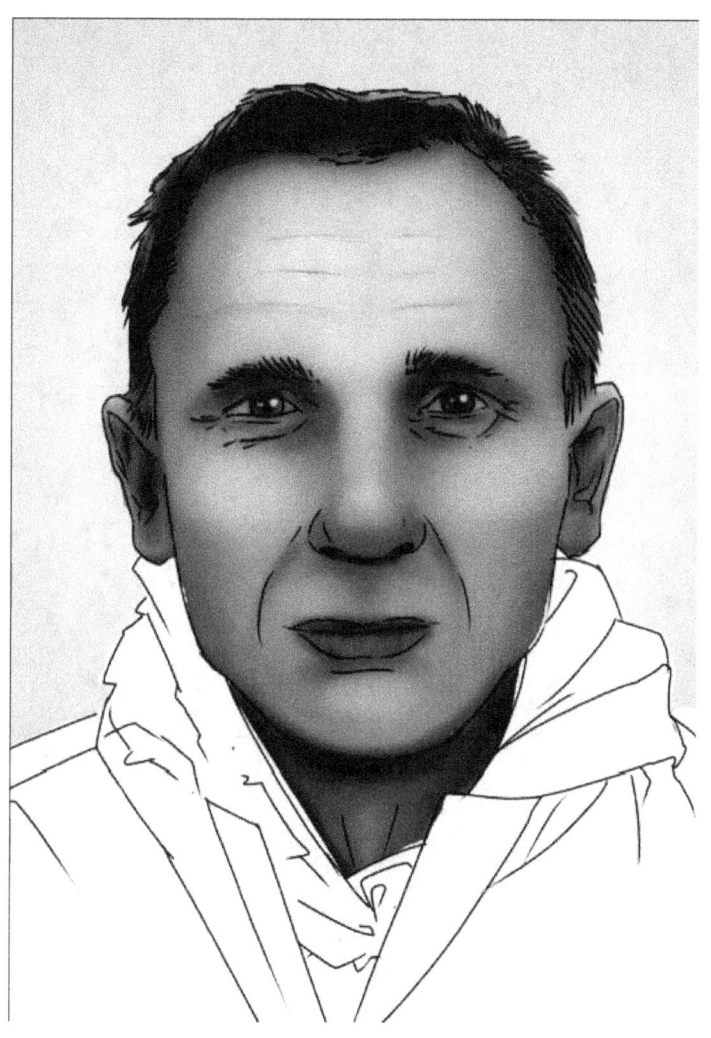

Step 14

Give shading in the collar of his jacket.

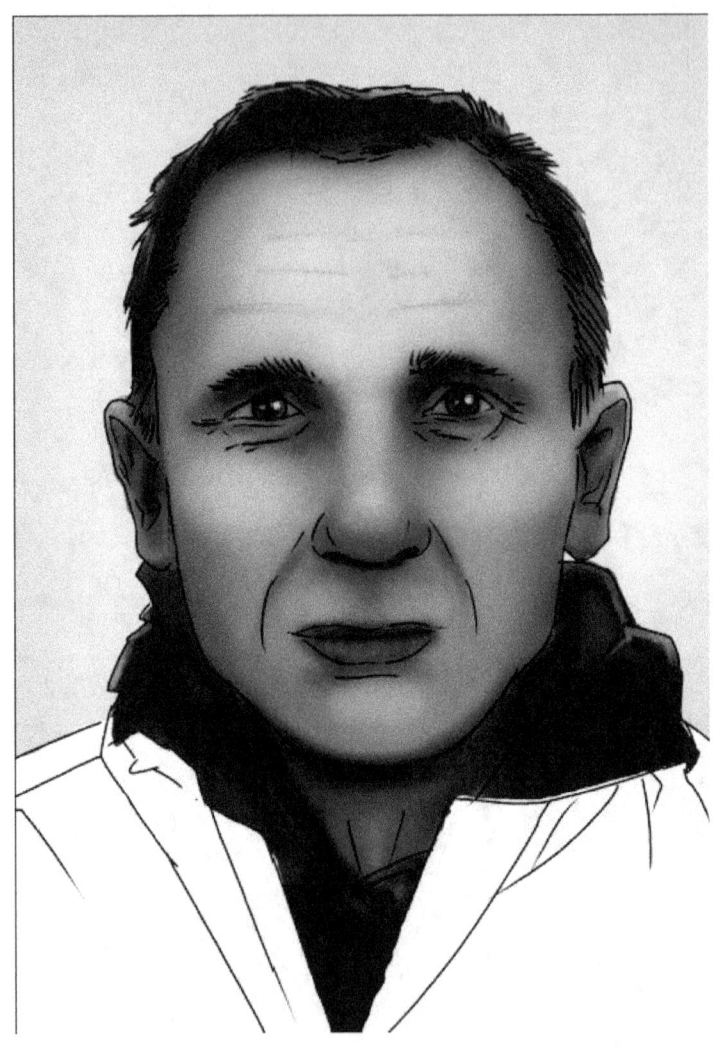

Step 15

Give shading in the remaining jacket, which is darker than the collar. The portrait of Alexis is complete.

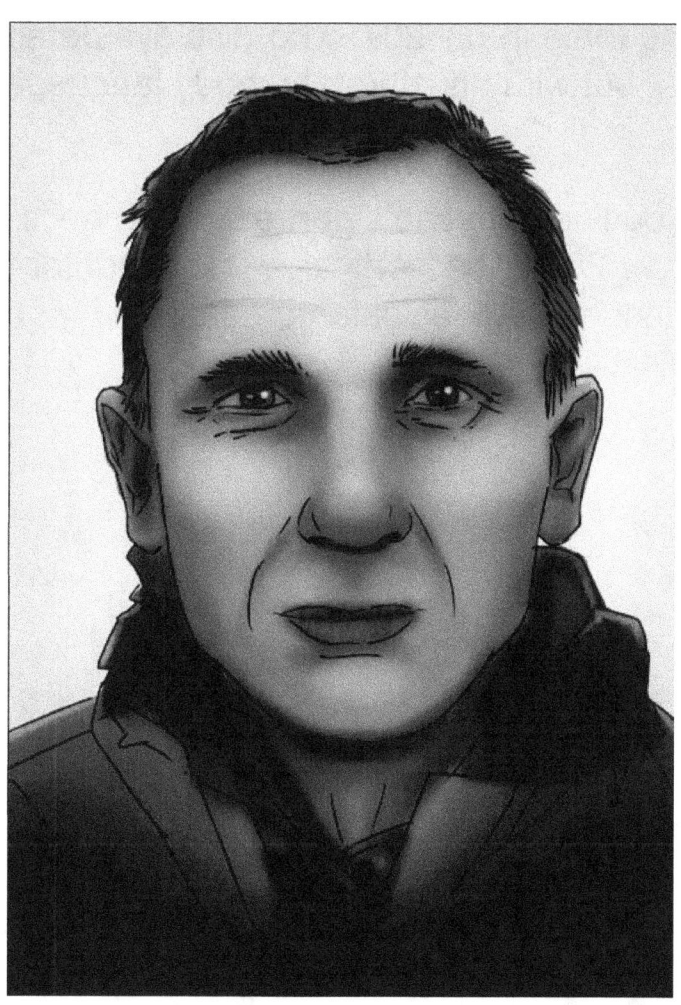

Chapter 7
Portrait of Jacob (male)

Jacob is a young male in his 20s, who displays details in his portrait not with his face, but with his attire and body language.

Step 1

Draw the basic outline of Jacob's portrait where he is standing a little tilted at his back. Draw the vertical and horizontal lines that were meant for the placement of facial features.

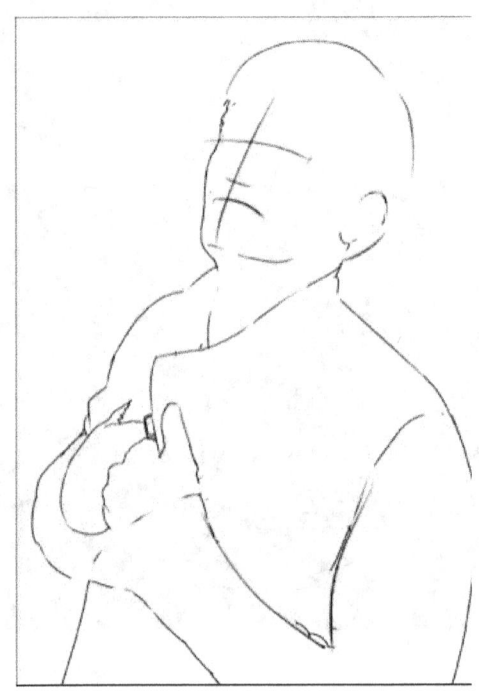

Step 2

Draw his hair's strands, which are dispersed in different directions. His hands are locked in his shirt as if he is trying to open the buttons of his shirt.

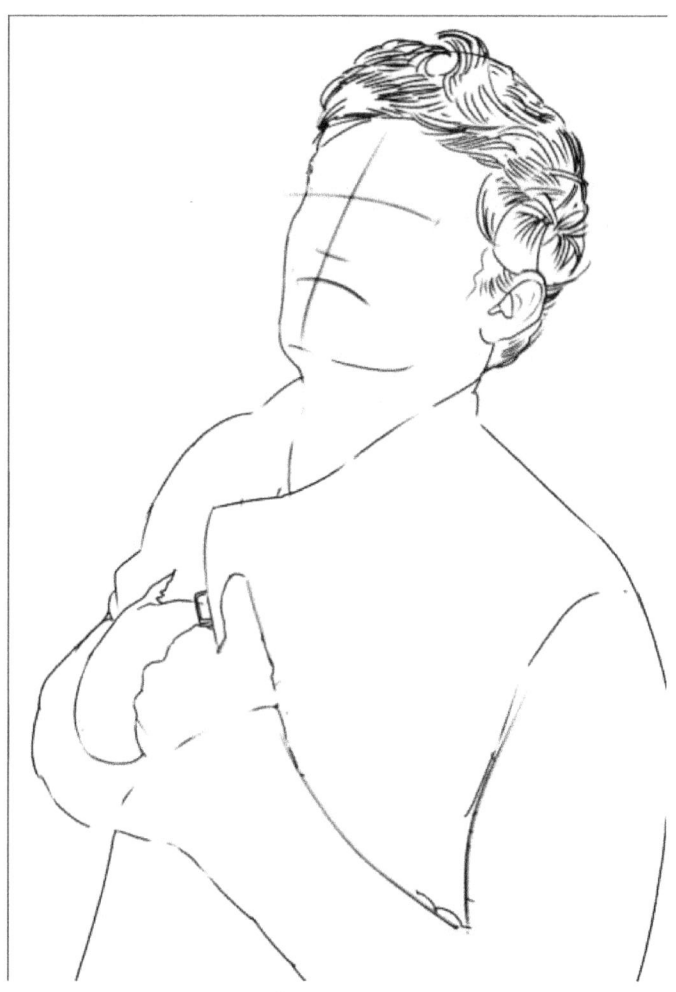

Step 3

Give details of his hands, including the nails, wrinkles, and nerves.

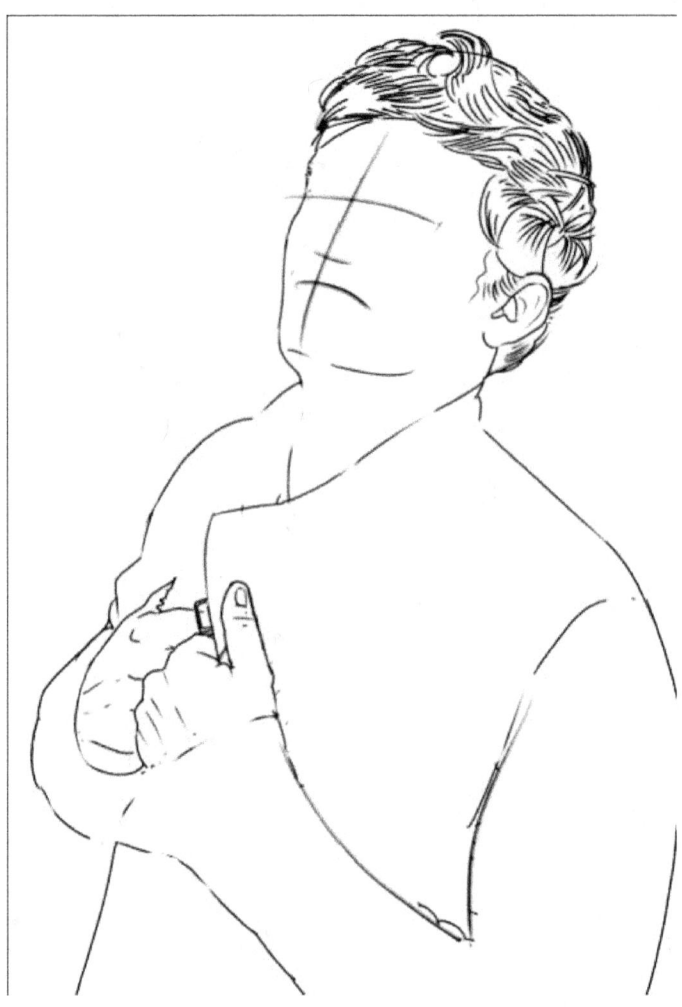

Step 4

Give details to his eyes, nose, lips, and ears.

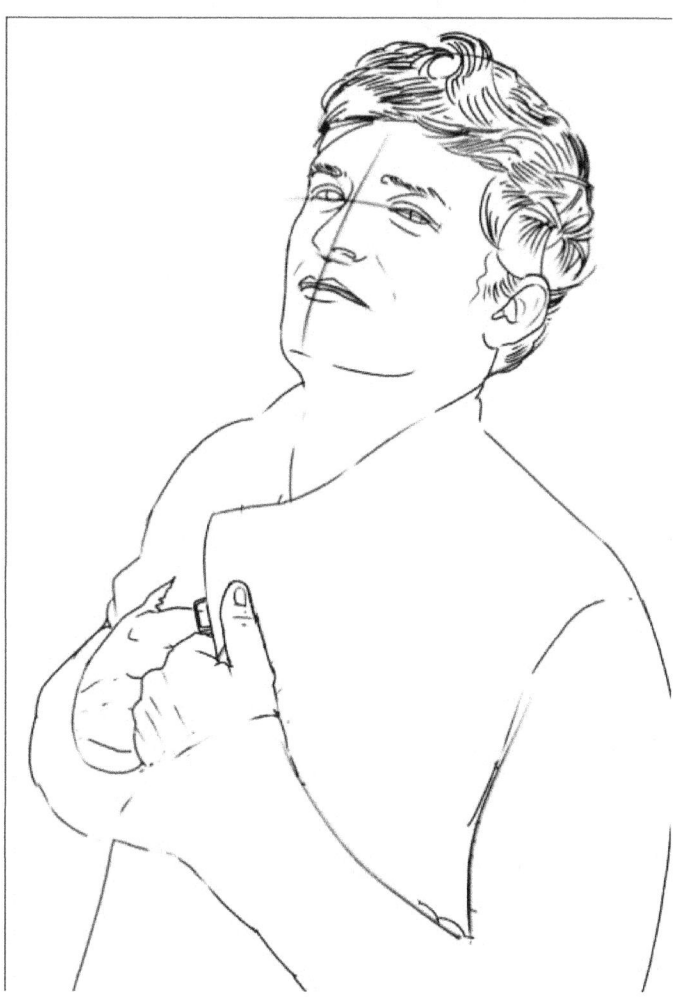

Step 5

Give details to his clothing such as a little fabric detailing on the sleeve hole and creases all around his jacket.

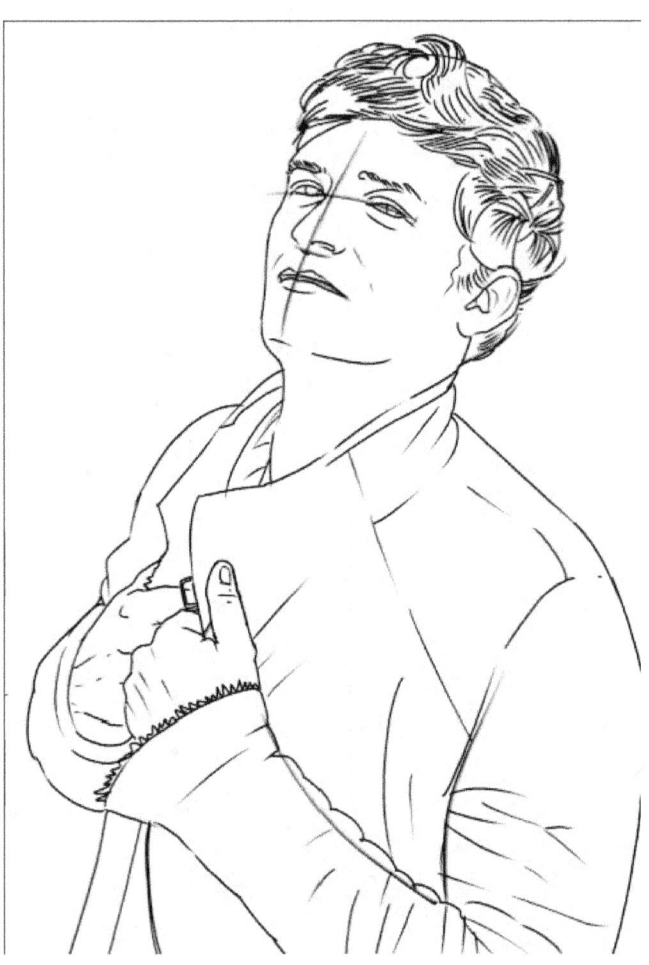

Step 6

Remove the vertical and horizontal lines that were meant for the placement of facial features.

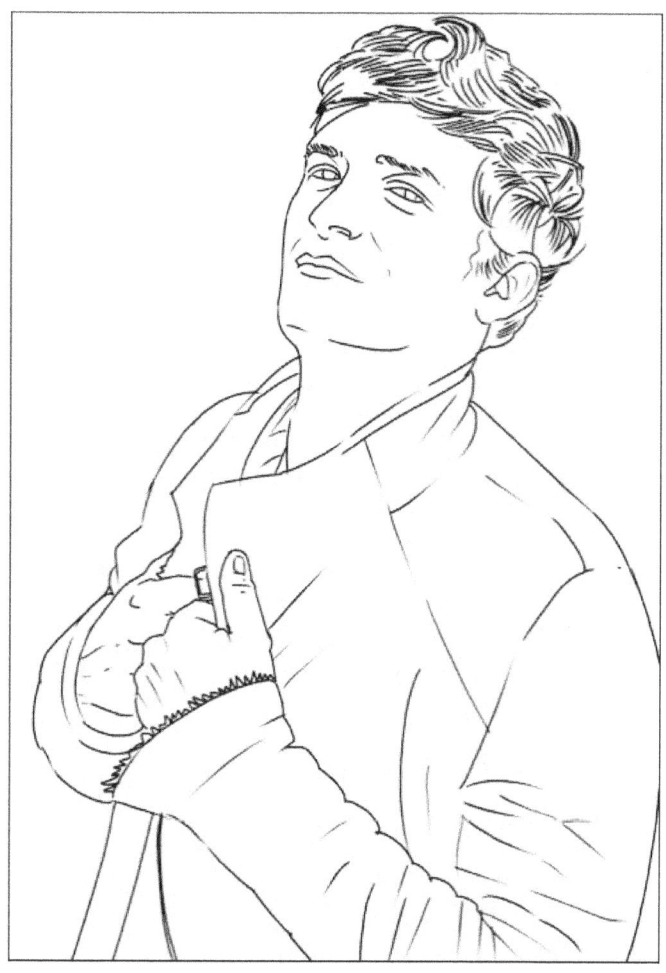

Step 7

Give light grey shading in the bottom left corner of the background of Jacob's portrait.

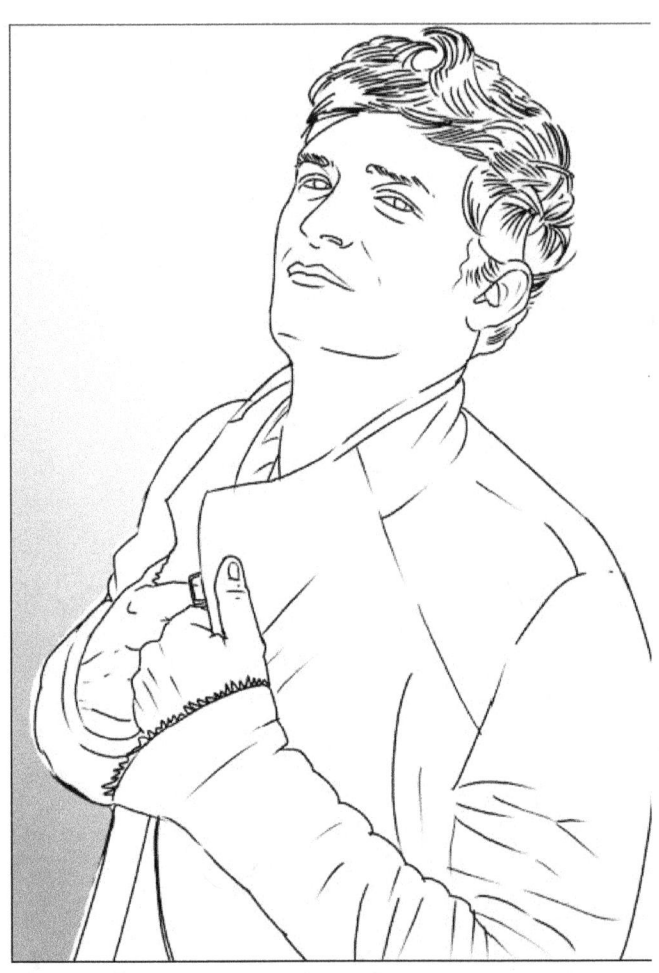

Step 8

Give shading in the clothes of Jacob.

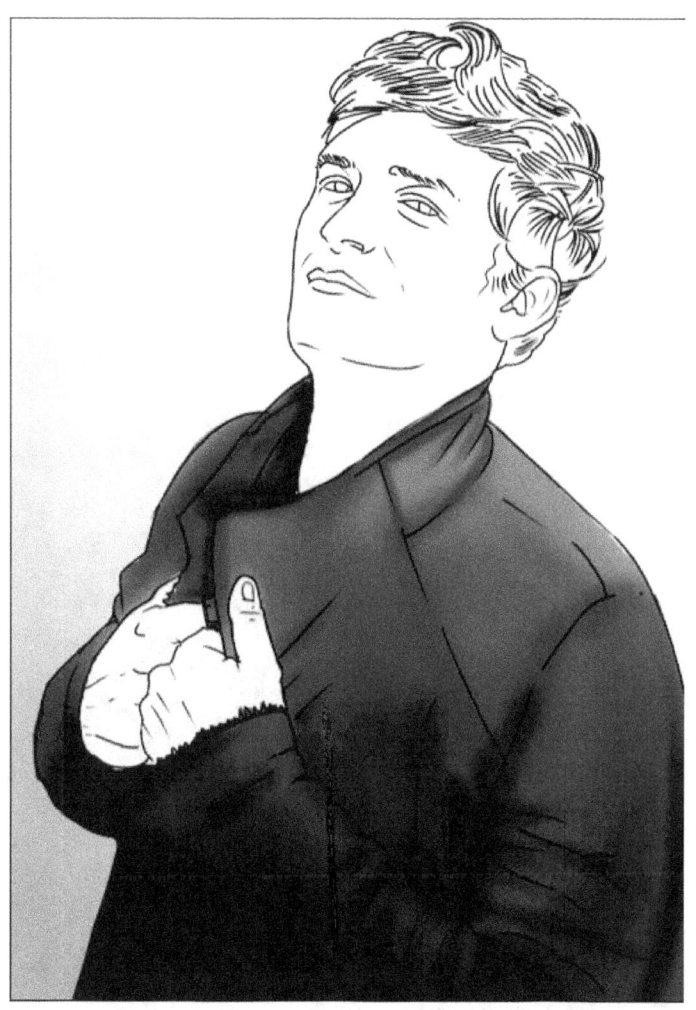

Step 9

Give shading in his hands.

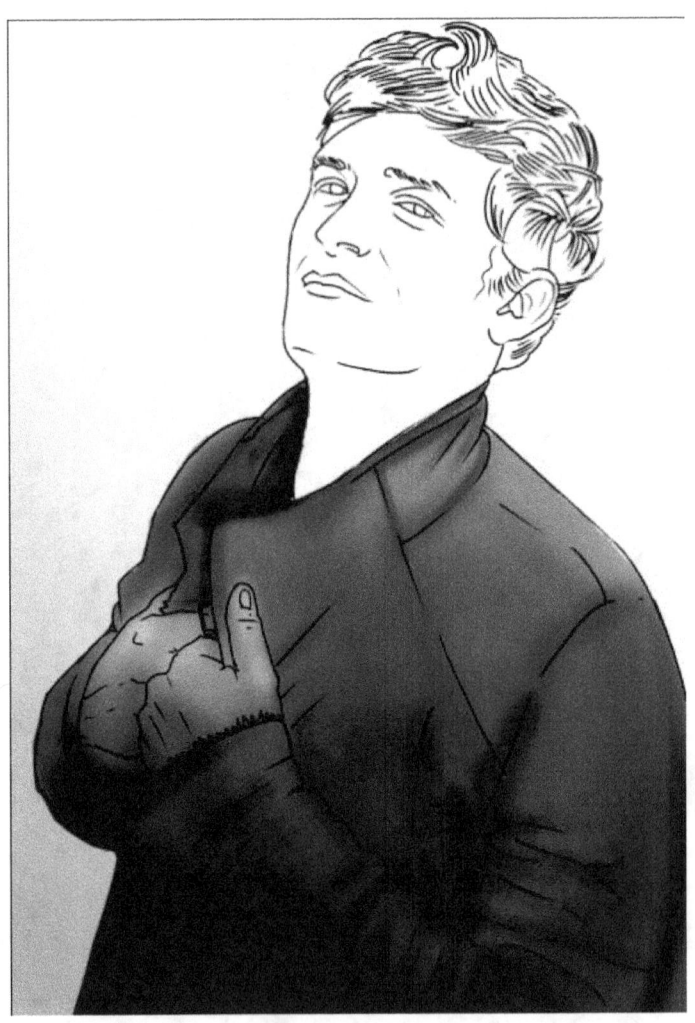

Step 10

Give shading in the face and ears of Jacob, leaving eyes, nose, and mouth.

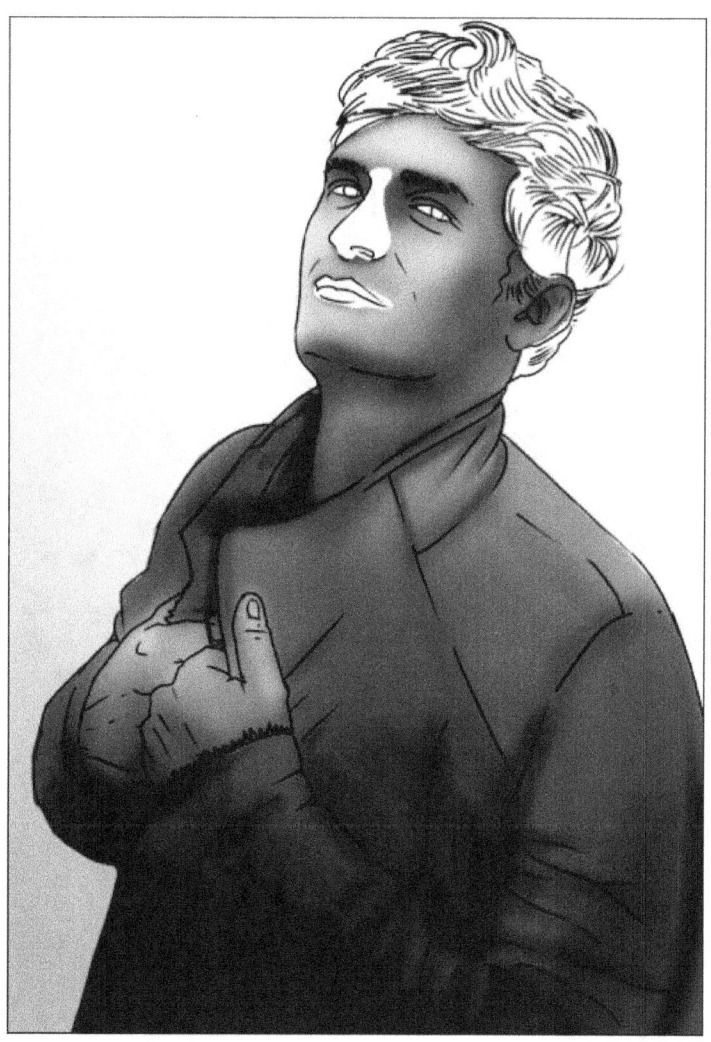

Step 11

Give shading in his hairs.

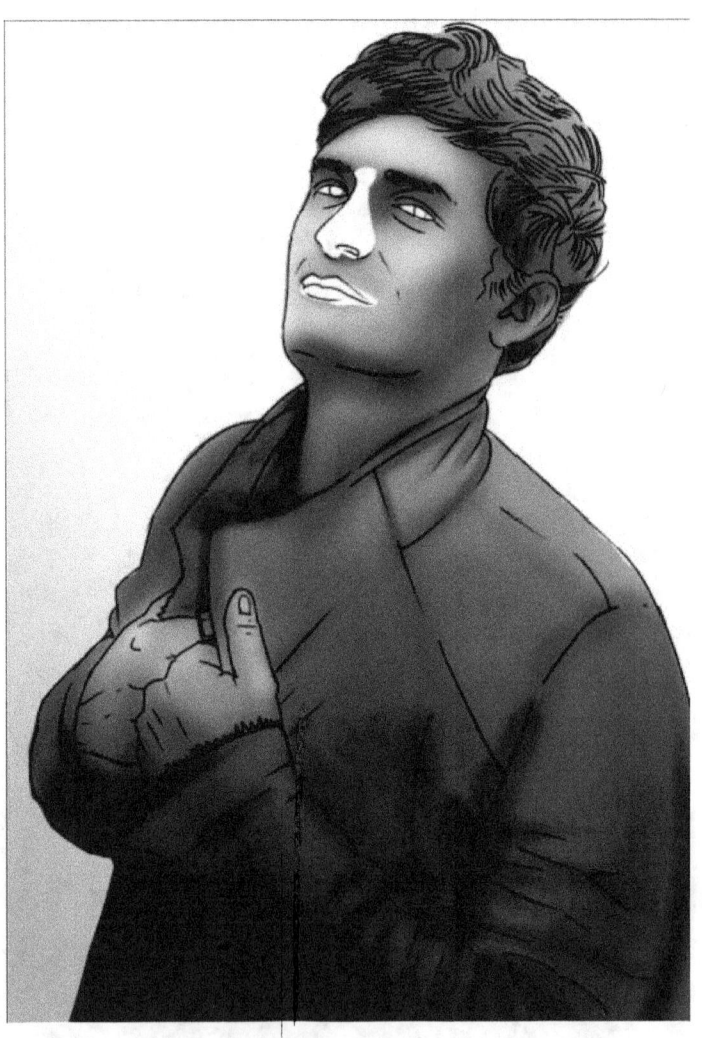

Step 12

Give shading in his eyes, nose, and mouth. Since he is not an old man, his face does not show many wrinkles. The portrait of Jacob is complete.

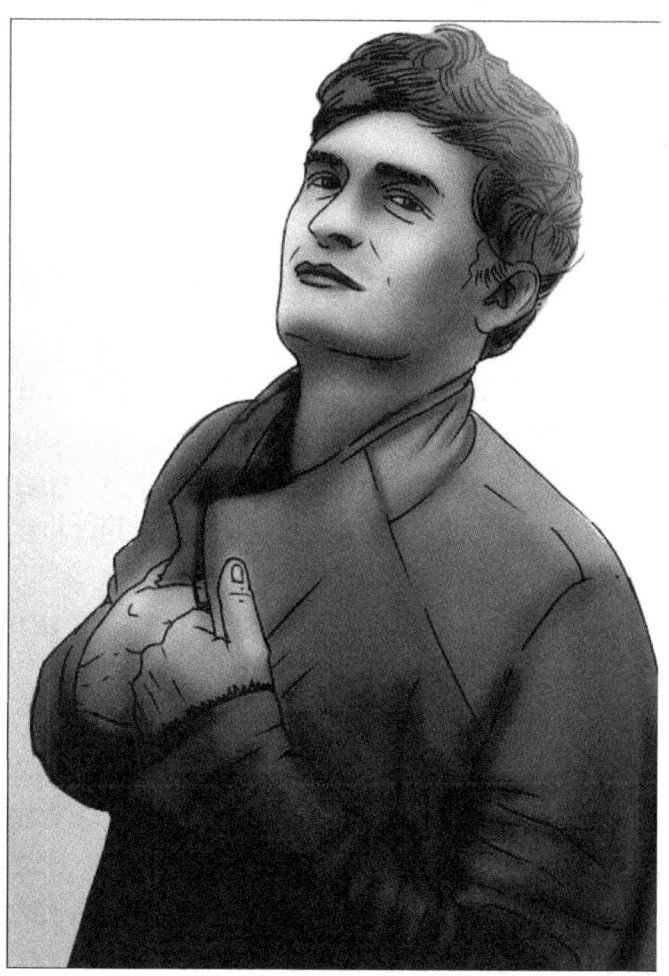

Conclusion

Portraits given in the illustrations of this book may seem relatively easy to you. Since these portraits are drawn with the help of computer software, you will have to double your efforts when you draw them with pencil and charcoal. The main idea of this book is to introduce you with the process of portrait drawing. The rest of the efforts are up to you.

You can read any number of books you want and go through any number of tutorials on YouTube. Everything is worthless unless you shed your hesitance, pick up the drawing equipment, and begin drawing. The first step is the only step that is difficult to take. You do not have to make much effort after that. Many people become expert in drawing the human body, but lag behind in drawing faces just because they are hesitant about achieving the likeliness.

A nonprofessional artist has a pre-set image of human face in their mind. When they try to draw the face, they try to draw a *perfect* nose, *perfect* eyes, *perfect* lips, and *perfect* everything in the face. However, the fact is that no human face is perfect or identical to each other. If you look around yourself, you will always find the most beautiful people in the world complaining about their face or body. Keeping this fact in mind, you just have to draw a face as you see in the picture. Do not try to perfect the portrait; it will spoil the originality of the person's face. Just draw what you see. If there is a black mole, or the eyebrows of a female are not identical, draw them as they are.

You will be amazed at the results you achieve. If you stop trying to perfect a portrait, you will get great results as they are meant to be. You can ask your friends and family to pose for you so that you can get free high- resolution images. If you get bored of drawing human faces, you can even draw your pets for a change. However, drawing animals is a completely different genre. But you have to take a break from everything sometimes. Do not feel bad if you feel saturated from drawing. Just take a breather, have some fresh air, and get back to work as soon as you can.

Finally, as it is stated many times before, you need to give deliberate practice to portrait drawing. No artist becomes great by creating art works once in a week. You have to fail a hundred times before you succeed once. Finally, when you succeed, your success speaks for your failures.